TIM
ANDERSON

RAMEN

FOREVER

ラーメン

TIM ANDERSON

RAMEN

FOREVER

ラーメンに命をかけて

RECIPES FOR RAMEN SUCCESS

Hardie Grant

BOOKS

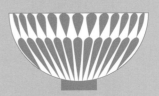

WHAT
IS
RAMEN?
ラーメンとは
なんですか？
RAMEN TO WA, NAN DESU KA?

4
PERFECT RAMEN IS THE FRIEND OF GOOD RAMEN

I am, in general, a fan of Voltaire's saying 'perfect is the enemy of good'. But in the case of ramen, the aphorism just isn't true. The pursuit of perfection – folly and futile though it may be – will inevitably result in an improved product and better understanding of your craft. So if you have a 'perfect' bowl in your mind, by all means, try to nail that bowl. You might not make it. I never have. But my ramen is getting better all the time. Embrace trial and error, and you'll steadily inch closer to realising your ramen dreams.

5
RAMEN IS EVERYTHING, AND EVERYTHING IS (OR CAN BE) RAMEN

Because of its simple, 'blank slate' format – as long as it contains alkaline wheat noodles in broth, it's ramen – anything can be made into ramen. And I would take it a step further and say: everything *should be* made into ramen. You will find, both in Japan and abroad, many absurd instances of ramen fusion dishes. This, I believe, comes from a conviction that ramen is the most perfect food and other foods would generally be improved if they could only be ramen.

However, just because everything can be ramen doesn't mean that everything automatically *is* ramen. Certain things are often mistaken for ramen but they are categorically NOT RAMEN and NOT RAMEN is NOT ALLOWED. Let me explain:

WHAT *ISN'T* RAMEN?

Ramen is, to some people, shorthand for just about any dish consisting of long noodles in broth. There are at least two instances where this is categorically incorrect:

1. Whenever non-ramen noodles are used. Ramen noodles are a specific type of noodle, characterised by their use of wheat flour and alkaline salts known as kansui (more details on page 67). Udon, soba and sōmen, for example, are not ramen. Rice noodles of any kind are *certainly* not ramen. Egg noodles (unless they also contain kansui) are also not ramen. You get the idea. No kansui, no ramen.

2. Whenever a ramen-like dish is already known as something else. I am thinking primarily of Chinese noodle soups here, which may fit the most basic criteria of ramen (alkaline noodles in broth) but go by other names and usually predate ramen. I do not know enough about Chinese cuisine to offer many specific examples, but one that does come to mind is wonton noodle soup. While wonton noodles are basically the same as ramen, calling them that would in my opinion amount to cultural reductionism and erasure (see also: sushi vs *gimbap*).

Other than that: anything goes. Got broth? Got noodles with a pH above seven? Guess what: you've got ramen!

RAMEN
AND
ME
ラーメンと私
RAMEN TO WATASHI

Ramen is my life force. I mean this very literally. Everything I am now, everything I do and everything I have, is because of ramen.

You may think I'm exaggerating – but it's absolutely true. Ramen was the impetus behind a number of huge, life-changing decisions for me. Allow me to explain, in timeline form:

2004

A chance visit to the family-run ramen shop Daikokuya in Los Angeles provides a revelatory ramen moment. I was enraptured by the dish, and became instantly obsessed with it.

2005

I am awarded a research grant to study regional noodle cultures in Japan. My research is focused on the Shin-Yokohama Ramen Museum, which further expands my understanding of the dish and fuels an urge to explore more of Japan – and eat more ramen.

2006

I am accepted onto the JET Program, a 'job' 'teaching' 'English' in Japan which was really just a means to go and learn more about Japanese food, especially ramen. On my application form, I chose all of my preferred placement locations based on ramen: Sapporo, Yokohama and Fukuoka. I am placed in Kitakyushu, Fukuoka Prefecture. If I hadn't moved there, I would never have met my wife, and therefore never moved to the UK, and never had our two wonderful children. The fact that the existence of my kids is predicated on my obsession with ramen is kind of crazy for me to think about.

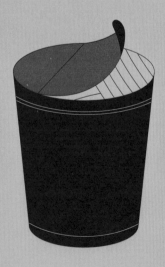

2011

I win *MasterChef*, in part by making ramen (with truffled lobster gyoza) for my main course in the final.

2013

I establish Nanban as a pop-up ramen izakaya restaurant, which later opened at a permanent site in Brixton in 2015.

2015

I publish my first cookbook, *Nanban: Japanese Soul Food*. The focus of this book is (you guessed it) regional ramen recipes.

2021

After six years, I leave the restaurant, partly because I am frustrated with my own failure to create and foster a kitchen environment that produces great ramen consistently.

My whole life would have been very, very different if it weren't for ramen. Wherever life has taken me, I got there by following ramen.

And yet, despite my many years of experience with ramen – as an eater, a student and a chef – I write this book with no small amount of trepidation. Writing a book about ramen feels like a fool's errand, an impossible task. Ramen is such an enormous topic that any ramen book will inevitably feel woefully incomplete. So just bear in mind that this book is completely inadequate in its scope, and you should not stop here in your ramen education. I have compiled further reading and resources on page 215.

However, what this book will do is provide a reasonably good understanding of the fundamental principles of ramen. You will still make mistakes making ramen. Ramen is hard. But whether you are a professional chef or an ambitious home cook, I hope this book will mitigate some of those mistakes and set you up for ramen success.

THE FIVE ELEMENTS OF RAMEN
ラーメンの5つ の要素
RAMEN NO ITSUTSU NO YŌSO

It is now commonly accepted that ramen contains five elements: broth, tare, noodles, aroma oil, and toppings. This book provides several recipes for each element, with recommendations for which other elements to pair them with listed alongside each recipe. These recommendations are just ideas – feel free to mix and match, but with a few rare exceptions, you will need all five elements in any given bowl.

SŪPU スープ

TARE タレ

MEN 麺

BROTH

I used to think broth was the most important part of ramen, but now I know better – there is no such thing; it's really about how everything comes together. But the broth coats everything, seasons everything and can be felt in every mouthful. Which is to say: it might not be the most important thing, but you've got to get it right.

TARE

Tare is the liquid used to season and flavour the broth, and even though it only accounts for typically 10–20% of the volume of the broth, it has a huge impact on its overall taste. This is because it must contain all of the salt and most of the umami in the bowl, and quite a lot of the aroma, too. For years I didn't use a tare – I thought my broth was too precious to season with anything other than straight-up salt. What a fool I was. Tare is essential.

NOODLES

I know I said there's no 'most important' part of ramen. But for real, noodles are the most important part of ramen. If the noodles aren't good, the bowl won't be good. Noodles are the vehicle for everything else, like a conveyor belt of flavour. Think of noodles like the frame of a house. If they aren't right, the whole thing falls apart.

KŌMI ABURA 香味油

 GUZAI 具材

OIL

An aroma oil or fat adds flavour and body to the broth, insulates the soup and makes it more satisfying as a meal. At its most basic, animal fats such as lard or schmaltz are used, and sometimes there is enough fat in the broth that additional oil is unnecessary. But for me, the oil is an opportunity to add extra complexity and evocative fragrance to the bowl – so don't miss that opportunity.

TOPPINGS

Ramen toppings are one of the trickiest elements to get right because they have the ability to throw the balance of the bowl out of whack, and if they aren't prepped thoughtfully, they interrupt slurpability. As a general rule, toppings should be easy to eat with chopsticks and interact well with noodles. So, for example, *chāshū* that falls apart quite eagerly is (in my opinion) preferable to leaner, chewier chāshū as it isolates itself from the noodles and must be eaten separately, in a non-slurpable way.

If you're in the UK, you can use a certain ramen chain as a reference point for how toppings should not be deployed. They contain huge chunks of chewy protein, extraneous piles of salad and reckless amounts of overpowering garnishes such as red onion and coriander (cilantro) leaves. But then, what do you expect from a chain that calls udon dishes ramen?

When in doubt with toppings, I think a good rule to live by is: less is more. Unless you're making Jirō-style ramen (page 169). Then more is more. A *lot* more.

TOOLS OF THE TRADE
ラーメン作り
の道具
RAMEN ZUKURI NO DŌGU

Generally speaking, ramen can be made in any ordinary kitchen with not much need for specialist equipment. However, there are a few things to point out, especially if you are a ramen professional.

POTS AND PANS

Obviously, you will need pots and pans of various sizes for making ramen. For broth and boiling noodles, you'll need big ones – at least 10 litres (338 fl oz) capacity, even for domestic-sized batches. If you're a professional chef, consider a stock pot with a false bottom and a tap near the base, which will assist with draining. For really large pots you will also need a stirring paddle, to redistribute ingredients and prevent burning on the bottom.

SIEVES, COLANDERS, SPIDERS AND BASKETS

First and foremost you'll need a good colander or spider and a fine sieve, for two-phase draining of broth (page 26). Noodle baskets are not essential for domestic kitchens but they are useful, so I'd get a few regardless.

SCALES AND MICROSCALES

Particularly for making noodles, you will need an accurate set of scales. For measuring kansui and salt in particular, which need to be weighed out to the gram, it is advisable to use microscales as they are more precise and sensitive.

THERMOMETERS

You will need a thermometer, the kind where the probe is attached by a cable, mainly for keeping an eye on the temperature of clear broths as they simmer. However, they are also useful for checking the doneness of chāshū (although I just go by feel for that sort of thing) as well as broths that are reheated or hot-held.

JUGS, LADLES AND MEASURING SPOONS

You'll need measuring jugs for checking the yields on broths as well as portioning out enough to reheat for service. A variety of accurate dosing ladles are essential – look online for 360 ml (12 fl oz), 300 ml (10 fl oz) and 30 ml (1 fl oz) ones to start with, as most ramen will contain between 300–400 ml (10–14 fl oz) of broth, plus 30–60 ml (1–2 fl oz) of tare. For fine-tuning things like tare and oil measurements, you can get Japanese 10 ml (2 teaspoons) or 5 ml (1 teaspoon) ladles, though these are hard to find outside of Japan. At home, our old friends the measuring spoons will do nicely instead.

KNIVES AND SAWS

Ramen doesn't generally require any fancy knifework, but you'll still want a good, sharp chef's knife or santoku knife for things like shredding spring onions (scallions) or thinly slicing chāshū. You may also want a heavy cleaver for dealing with bones, but be warned: I have broken many a cleaver when trying to smash through tough pork bones and joints. If your butcher won't do this for you, get yourself a decent hacksaw and a hammer.

WHISKS, BLENDERS AND FOOD PROCESSORS

Whisks, mainly small-ish ones, are important particularly for mixing thick tare (such as miso or tantan) evenly into broths. Likewise, a good stick blender is essential for similar work, but also for re-emulsifying broths. A good food processor is also useful, for everything from blending tare and grinding sesame seeds, to mincing loads of garlic for Jirō-style ramen.

STORAGE CONTAINERS

Because ramen involves so much *mise en place*, it involves a lot of containers of various sizes. You'll probably need to invest in some very large ones (3 litre/101 fl oz) capacity or so) for broth, and wide, shallow ones are preferable to tall, narrow ones, to expedite cooling.

KEY POINT

In this book I have used a mixture of weights and volumetric measurements. For the most part, this is just how I cook intuitively, but often it is done deliberately so things are easier to measure and scale. For noodles, only metric weights are used; this is due to the precise nature of these recipes. Ounces simply won't work.

A BRIEF GUIDE TO INGREDIENTS
材料の基本的な案内
ZAIRYŌ NO KIHONTEKI NA ANNAI

I could write a whole book just about ramen ingredients, and that's no exaggeration. There's a lot that goes into ramen, and a lot to say about all of it. I discuss specific ingredients more within particular chapters and recipes, but for now there are just a few things I'd like to flag.

BONES, MEAT AND OTHER ANIMAL PARTS

You can certainly make ramen from any bones you can get, but using good ones will make a massive difference to your finished broth. Above all else, make sure the bones are fresh – butchers don't usually get through them very fast so they might be on the turn by the time they get to you.

MENTSUYU/ SHIRODASHI

These concentrated Japanese soup stocks don't appear in many recipes, but they are extremely useful to have on hand for making ramen. Both are essentially noodle soup seasonings, which makes them perfect for ... seasoning noodle soup. They are an excellent 'shortcut' tare, especially when checking the flavour of your broth as it comes to the end of its cook. They also make a good, quick marinade for boiled eggs, though because they are so salty, you should dilute them with a little bit of water and perhaps mirin before adding the eggs.

SOY SAUCE

Most recipes that use soy sauce call for *shōyu*, which is Japanese, naturally brewed, all-purpose soy sauce. I have avoided calling for super-specific types of soy sauce, but some recipes do use *usukuchi* ('light' soy sauce) or tamari, so make sure you've got the right kind in those instances. If you can get them, I highly recommend unpasteurised (*nama*) soy sauces, which I think are more complex and more vibrant.

FLOUR

All of the noodle recipes here call for strong white bread flour, and what kind you use doesn't matter that much, but I would recommend just sticking to one brand. Flours have a lot of variation in terms of their protein content, how they hydrate, etc., so you may find that you have to adjust a recipe when you've switched to a different flour, even if you've already fine-tuned it and it worked before.

MISO

As with soy sauce, I have avoided specific regional varieties or brands, but I do call for specific types. I assume some familiarity with miso here, so read up on it if you're not sure.

MIRIN, SAKE AND RICE VINEGAR

I have used a mid-range hon-mirin (real mirin) for all of the recipes here, which provides a pleasant but unobtrusive aroma. I would not recommend using a premium hon-mirin for most recipes, which tend to be too strongly flavoured, nor a cheap 'mirin-style seasoning', which are too weak. On a related note, sake should just be basic cooking sake – nothing expensive. 'Vinegar' refers to ordinary rice vinegar unless others are specifically called for.

HOW TO IMPROVE YOUR RAMEN
ラーメンを美味しく する方法
RAMEN WO OISHIKU SURU HŌHŌ

TINKER

Ramen didn't turn out quite how you wanted it to? It rarely does. Keep tweaking your recipe and fine-tuning your technique until you get there. Check your ingredients, too: tasty ingredients give you a better shot at tasty ramen. Often the difference between good ramen and great ramen is down to minute details, and it will take a long time, and lots of tinkering, to get them all pinned down.

TAILOR

Using other people's tried-and-tested recipes is a reliable way to make good ramen, but it won't be *your* ramen until you tailor it to your own tastes. Once you have a handle on the basics, ask yourself what you really want from a bowl. Refined, distinct flavours, clear broths, delicate noodles? Or maybe a devastating salvo of salt, lard and garlic, with noodles as tough as nails? Somewhere in between? Only you know what your 'perfect' bowl is like, so ultimately, only you know how to make it.

SOLDIER

It will probably take you a long time to get even passably good at making ramen. Take it from a guy who's been doing it for a decade and still considers himself an amateur: be prepared to start finding things to improve in bowls you once thought were practically perfect. Solider on, and keep reaching for that ramen rainbow. After all, you'll still get to crush some bodacious bowls along the way.

SPY

Because everybody makes ramen in a slightly different way, there is an enormous wealth of ideas and techniques to draw upon – you just have to discover them. Get to know other ramen dorks and don't be afraid to ask questions. Peek into the kitchens of ramen shops you love. Ask them for a job. Go to Japan. Slurp, watch, learn – this is the ramen chef's eat, pray, love.

1

BROTHS

スープ

In a way, making broth is the easy part of making ramen. You whack some bones in a pot, you boil 'em, you got broth. Boom. However, in another, more accurate way, making broth is the hard part – it's a laborious, time-consuming, often dispiriting process with infinite variations and almost as many ways of going wrong.

So, before we get into specific recipes, I want to provide some general information and guidance on broth-making. Understanding the elements of broths and how they behave during cooking will get you closer to your broth goals from the get-go.

CHINTAN
VS PAITAN
清湯と白湯
CHINTAN TO PAITAN

Ramen soups are divided into two categories, *chintan* and *paitan*: clear broths and cloudy broths, respectively. Of course, this really ought to be thought of as a spectrum rather than a dichotomy, with pristinely clear, consommé-like chintan on one end and murky, fatty, opaque paitan on the other, and a full range of consistencies in between. Job one is deciding what kind of broth you're after, and more to the point, what kind of flavour profile you want to achieve.

The viscosity and appearance of the broth is mostly determined by the time and temperature of the boil, as well as the prep and handling of the bones. Let's say you've got a kilo of pork neck bones, a kilo of pork femurs, a kilo of chicken frames and half a kilo of chicken feet. If you were to put them all together and boil them hard for 8 hours, you'd have a pretty standard paitan, totally cloudy with a milky consistency. If you instead simmered them at 85°C (185°F) for the same amount of time, you'd have a chintan, albeit a hazy and fairly gelatinous one with a good slick of fat on its surface.

This is because broth cloudiness is caused by particles of fat and protein suspended in the water; a vigorous boil not only extracts more of both, it also churns them up so they naturally emulsify within the broth and make it opaque. Now, if you were to take that chintan made from the same bones and mix it up – say, by overenthusiastic stirring or straining – that movement would cloud the broth. You wouldn't call it a paitan, as that would require both more fat and more intense blending, but it would be noticeably hazier. It is also worth noting that, if you leave a paitan to settle, the inverse isn't really true: most of its fat will naturally separate out over time, but the liquid itself won't clarify and become a chintan. Once a paitan, always a paitan.

However, it's not all about how you cook and handle your broths. Certain bones – or other animal parts – are better for certain things than others, so your bone bill should be tailored to the kind of broth you want to make.

SELECTING YOUR BONES (AND OTHER BITS)
骨と他の材料の選択
HONE TO HOKA NO ZAIRYŌ NO SENTAKU

Bones provide three main things to broth: collagen, fat and flavour.

COLLAGEN

All broths, whether paitan or chintan, require a good amount of collagen, which dissolves in the boil to make gelatine and gives the broth body. This allows it to cling to noodles and coat toppings, and it also provides a lip-smacking, satisfying mouthfeel. Broths with insufficient gelatine feel watery and hollow, which is why for many years I resisted making plant-based broths. (I later realised there are other ways to add body – page 37.) Collagen is found most abundantly in cartilage and connective tissue, which is why active joints like feet, wings, tails and skulls make for good broth.

FAT

A good amount of fat is essential in paitan, contributing to its creamy richness as well as its opaque, whitish appearance. Paitan without enough fat are sad and thin, which is why they usually contain lots of bone marrow from pork femurs, chicken skin and the like. Fat is not desirable in chintan, so these kinds of cuts should be avoided, but there will inevitably be at least a little bit of fat to contend with. Not to worry – it can be skimmed off and used later as an aroma oil.

FLAVOUR

This is the tricky one. What we think of as flavour is actually a combination of basic tastes and what are known as retronasal olfactory aromas, which is to say, things we're able to smell when they're already in our mouths. The main taste we're after in ramen broth is umami – more on that later (page 47), but for now all I'll say is that it really accounts for very little of what we perceive to be the overall flavour of the broth. That's actually all aroma.

Here's the annoying thing: capturing aroma is sort of inherently at odds with the broth-making process, because as you sustain the heat of the liquid over an extended amount of time, you naturally vaporise volatile aroma compounds and lose them, never to be smelled again. Is your broth starting to smell good as it ticks away on the stovetop? Well, the bad news is that means your broth is actually *losing* aroma as it's developing it. If it's in your nose, it's not in the pot and therefore it won't make it into the bowl. It may go without saying that chintan, which are cooked at lower temperatures, are generally better at preserving aroma compounds, because fewer are vaporised or destroyed through boiling. An even better way to preserve flavour is by making broth in the microwave (page 44) – but this is lousy at extracting gelatine.

So there's always a trade-off, unfortunately. This is mostly a problem in paitan, where the very long, high-temperature boils required to extract sufficient fat and gelatine inevitably result in the loss of meaty aroma. However, you can correct for this in a few ways. One is by shortening the boil, which is made possible by choosing cuts in which the joints are smaller and therefore break down faster, such as chicken feet. Cutting up pork femurs and trotters to expose their marrow helps as well. You can also just whack in a lot of back fat as a shortcut. But if these options are not possible, or don't give you the results you want, then late bone additions will help replenish some of the aroma that's been boiled away. Similarly, when making paitan – tonkotsu especially – vegetables or other aromatic ingredients should be added in the last 1–2 hours of the boil or their flavour will be totally gone by the time the broth is pulled off the heat.

Whatever kind of broth you want to make, consider what kind of bones and cuts will give you the right balance of the above elements. You may find this Venn diagram helpful, which categorises various parts by what they're best at delivering:

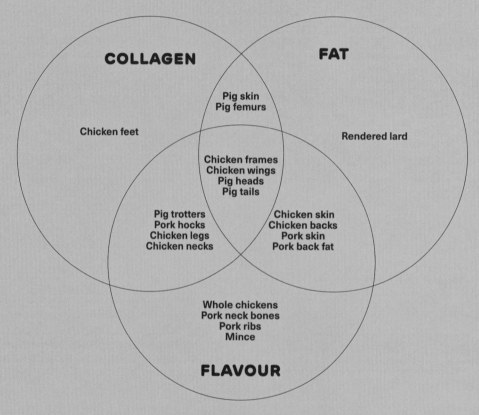

A quick caveat on the above: all animal parts contribute flavour, of course, and the ones that deliver flavour in the form of fat or marrow will retain aroma compounds better in the long run. The parts listed in the 'flavour' circle are ones that best express the meaty aroma of, you know, actual meat. So if you want a broth that really tastes like chicken, use a whole chicken; if you want a really porky broth, use ribs, etc. Just remember to either keep them at a low temperature for a long time to make chintan, or add them later in the boil of a paitan.

Of course, if it's flavour you're after – and duh, it is – then it's important that the bones are relatively fresh. Not sure about the condition of your bones? Give 'em a good sniff. Chicken bones should have virtually no smell when raw; pork might be a little funky, but not a lot. It may also go without saying that the better quality the animals, the better the bones, and therefore the better the broth – though this is much more noticeable with chicken than it is with pork. Broth from bad chicken tastes of next to nothing; broth from good chicken is sweet and rich and beautiful.

If you want a really luscious pork flavour, it's best to use basic bones and then finish the bowl with lard rendered from top-quality rare-breed pigs, or infuse it with Iberico ham or top-quality bacon. (If you know any Spanish chefs, ask them if you can have the bones from their hams – dashi made from these is really something.)

DE-GUNKING: ROASTING, BLANCHING, SKIMMING AND SOAKING
あくの取り方
AKU NO TORIKATA

BOILING VS SIMMERING
スープ作りの適切温度
SŪPU TSUKURI NO TEKISETSU ONDO

For any broth, you first need to remove the blood from the bones, which would otherwise create a dark, dingy soup with a muddy, metallic flavour. Probably the easiest way to do this is to roast the bones. The heat will boil and therefore congeal the blood and other protein, which means it won't taint the broth and it has the added benefit of rendering fat and developing additional flavour compounds.

An alternative method is to blanch the bones first, which draws out the blood quickly and sets it so it can be easily washed away. To do this, place the bones into a pot covered with cool water and bring to the boil. For small bones such as chicken, you can then drain and rinse the bones immediately; for thicker pork bones and the like, leave them to boil for about 10 minutes so the heat fully penetrates them. The main benefit of this method is that it will result in a lighter-coloured broth – but if that's not a priority, I'd stick with roasting.

Two final options for de-gunking your bones are skimming and soaking. To remove the blood by skimming, simply place the bones in a pot and proceed to make broth as per the recipe, but skim any scum that floats to the surface with a fine sieve or shallow ladle as the water comes to the boil. This method is quite hands-on, at least for the first hour or so, when most of the scum forms. You can reduce the amount of scum by soaking the bones in cold water overnight, but this method is imperfect – there will still be skimming to do.

I have been using the word 'boil' with reckless abandon, when really I should be saying 'cook', because not all broths are boiled. Chintan are just simmered, or not even, but held at a sub-simmering temperature. And this is when you want to bust out the thermometer. For paitan, it doesn't really matter – you just need to keep it bubbling away, not at a crazy fierce boil on your biggest burner or anything, but rolling steadily the whole time. Use a lid to maintain heat efficiently, but if you do, leave a space of about 2.5 cm (1 in) between the surface of the broth and the rim of the pot, to prevent spattering.

For chintan, keep the broth at around 85–90°C (185–194°F). This is hot enough to render a good amount of gelatine but not so hot that it causes excess fat and protein to cloud the broth. Don't stir chintan broths or this will cause them to cloud up; do stir paitan broths to break up bits of fat and connective tissue and to ensure that the bones aren't catching on the bottom of the pan.

FINISHING, STRAINING, CHILLING AND STORING

How do you know when your broth is done? We used to have a test at the restaurant: when we tasted it and it no longer tasted like water, it was done. This is admittedly imprecise, but isn't that all that really matters? Some chefs use a refractometer to measure the viscosity of the broth, but I simply never really found this necessary. But, by all means, if you want to fine-tune your broths or ensure absolute consistency from batch to batch, get yourself a refractometer.

Whatever your method for judging the broth's doneness, how it is handled after cooking is important, too. First of all: strain it. I do this in two phases, first by separating the bones out using a spider or colander. With chintan I opt for the spider, so I can remove most of the solids carefully before ladling the liquid through a sieve, minimising turbulence and therefore preserving clarity. With paitan this doesn't matter; just dump it through a colander, then through a sieve. (If you go straight into the sieve, the bones will pile up and the broth will spatter everywhere.)

If you're not using it right away, chill the broth down as quickly as you can to prevent microbial spoilage. The best way for most cooks to do this is by tipping it into a wide, shallow container such as a baking tray, letting it cool to room temperature, then transferring it, uncovered, to the refrigerator to chill completely. (If you are a ramen professional you will probably want to invest in a blast chiller, because it is otherwise very, very difficult to cool large batches of broth efficiently.) If you've made chintan, when the broth is completely cold and set, remove any fat that congeals on its surface.

Properly cooled broth will last for about a week in the refrigerator. Broth also freezes well – just use it within a few months. It should be noted that chintan which have been frozen or kept very cold may develop 'chill haze', a cloudiness that comes from proteins precipitating at very low temperatures, but don't be alarmed – this effect will be mostly reversed by reheating.

REHEATING AND EMULSIFYING

Most broths reheat fairly well, but repeated reheating or hot holding at too high of a temperature is very detrimental. If you are hot holding, do it at around 90–95°C (194–205°F) to minimise reduction and loss of aroma. If you're reheating to order, bring the broth back to a low boil just before dropping in the noodles. Paitan will need to be re-emulsified if you want it to have that lovely pearly white appearance. You can do this by boiling vigorously, but I wouldn't recommend it because of how it alters the broth's flavour and consistency. Instead, use a stick blender to whisk it all back together.

YIELDS

Yields in each recipe are an approximation, but your results shouldn't be that far off them – if they differ by 10% or more, consider adjusting the volume by topping up with water or reducing as needed. But what really matters is the taste – if you like it, ignore my yields and go with it!

豚骨スープ
Tonkotsu Sūpu

Tonkotsu

Tonkotsu is a paitan of pork bones, and for many it is the soup that gets them hooked on ramen – the gateway broth. Its rich consistency, concentrated meatiness and whiff of pigsty funk has a certain visceral appeal, though the same characteristics that make it beguiling to some make it off-putting to others.

For something that is nothing more than boiled bones, tonkotsu is surprisingly tricky to get right. One thing that has always vexed me about tonkotsu is that the meatiest pork aroma seems to arrive about 3–4 hours into the boil, after which it begins to dissipate. But 3–4 hours is not enough time to extract the right amount of fat and collagen and fully infuse the broth with the rich flavour of the marrow. To correct for this, this recipe uses a relatively short boil, with leaner, meatier pork added towards the end of that boil to preserve its aroma.

You may have read about pork broths being boiled for extremely long amounts of time – 18 hours, 24 hours, even 60 hours, with extra bone additions on the second and third days. For me, going over 12 hours is unnecessary, but it depends on what bones you choose and what you want in terms of flavour. During really extended boils, the bones themselves start to break down and you end up with a very deep, earthy flavour, especially if you use skulls. You may also end up with sandy little bits of obliterated bone in the bowl – which is not necessarily a fault. In fact, it is a key characteristic of Kurume ramen, considered one of the best and oldest examples of tonkotsu in Japan.

Paitan broths such as tonkotsu are commonly described as either *assari* or *kotteri* – light or rich respectively. This recipe results in a fairly kotteri broth – pretty fatty and quite sticky with gelatine. However, you can add more water to the finished broth if you prefer it lighter. (Don't worry too much about diluting the flavour – it will still be pretty strong, and anyway, a good *shio* (salt) tare will make everything feel more fortified and focused.)

→

Makes ≈2.4 litres (81 fl oz)
Total cook time: 10 hours

1.5 kg (3 lb 5 oz) pork femur
bones, split

1 kg (2 lb 4 oz) pork trotters,
split (roughly 2 medium)

1 rack (about 600–750 g/1 lb 5 oz–
1 lb 10 oz) pork spare ribs or neck
bones (or similar lean, meaty bones)

≈4 litres (135 fl oz) water,
plus extra for blanching

3 large (10–12 g/0.35–0.4 oz total)
dried shiitake mushrooms

2 garlic bulbs, halved

1 leek, coarsely chopped

1 apple, quartered

½ teaspoon ground white pepper

Blanch the bones according to the guide on page 25. Place all of the bones except the ribs into the pot, then add the water (enough to cover). With a lid on the pot, bring to a rolling boil and maintain it for 7 hours, stirring occasionally and topping up with water to maintain a consistent level as needed. After 7 hours, add the ribs and shiitake to the pot and continue to boil for 1 hour. (At this point, you may want to excavate the marrow manually; see Key Point below.) Then add the garlic, leek, apple and pepper, and continue to boil for 2 more hours. Remove from the heat, then strain, chill and store according to the guide on page 26, or bring back to a high simmer if using immediately. Remember to re-emulsify the broth with an immersion blender before serving.

KEY POINT

It is crucial that the femur bones are split open. Without doing this, the marrow inside them cannot be coaxed out except through extremely long boils. It is rare, in my experience, for butchers to split them lengthways (because of concerns about bandsaw safety), but this is the best option, as it exposes more marrow. If your butcher cuts the bones widthways (that is, across the diameter of the bone rather than down its length), it is worth excavating the marrow manually. To do this, allow the bones to boil for about 6–7 hours, at which point the marrow will be soft and squishy. Use tongs to fish out pieces of femur from the broth, then use a chopstick or the handle of a spoon to dig out the marrow and release it into the broth. This is not practical for large-scale boils, so if you are a ramen professional, your best bets are to get the femurs cut lengthways, cut into smaller chunks, or to extend your boil until the marrow melts out naturally.

スープ

Chicken Paitan

鶏白湯スープ
Tori Paitan Sūpu

This is essentially the chicken equivalent of tonkotsu, a rich, creamy soup which tastes like the happiest of mediums between a broth and a roast chicken gravy. While it's almost as fatty and gelatinous, chicken paitan doesn't have that faint whiff of death that tonkotsu has, just pure, powerful chickeny flavour. Chicken paitan also has one of the highest deliciousness-to-effort ratios among ramen broths: because chicken parts are so small compared to pork parts, you can fully extract their fat, flavour and gelatine in a fraction of the time it takes to make tonkotsu.

TARE
Any

NOODLES
Any

OILS
Allium and Ginger
 Schmaltz
Garlic Sesame
Nori

RAMEN
Tokyo Modern
Double Soup

Makes ≈2.4 litres (81 fl oz)
Total cook time: 6 hours

2 tablespoons vegetable oil or animal fat

50 g (1.75 oz) fresh ginger root, thinly sliced

1 onion, quartered

1 garlic bulb, halved

250 g (8.8 oz) chicken skin

250 g (8.8 oz) chicken feet

800 g (1 lb 12 oz) chicken wings

1.5 kg (3 lb 5 oz) chicken frames, roughly chopped

≈3.5 litres (118 fl oz) water

4 bay leaves (optional)

½ teaspoon white pepper

Heat the oil or fat in a roasting tray in a fan oven set to 200°C (425°F), then add all of the vegetables and chicken parts and roast for 40 minutes, turning everything once halfway through cooking. Remove the vegetables with tongs and set aside. Tip the chicken parts and any drippings from the tray into a stock pot and add the water (enough to cover) and bay leaves, and set over a high heat. Boil hard for 4 hours, topping up the water as needed to maintain the water level. After 4 hours add the veg and the white pepper, and continue to boil for another 2 hours. In the final hour, stop topping up the water and allow it to reduce slightly. Remove from the heat, then strain, chill and store according to the guide on page 26, or bring back to a high simmer if using immediately. Remember to re-emulsify the broth with an immersion blender before serving.

スープ

焼き豚骨と鶏ガラ 清湯スープ

Roast Pork and Chicken Chintan

Yaki Tonkotsu to Torigara Chintan Sūpu

This is a good go-to clear broth, based on a recipe I originally developed while trying to recreate the ramen at Harukiya, one of Tokyo's most iconic shops, which represents the perfect marriage of meaty aroma with soy saucy depth.

TARE
Any shio
Any shōyu
Bottled mentsuyu/
  shirodashi

NOODLES
Go-To
Springy-Chewy
Soba-Ramen
  Hybrid

OILS
Allium and Ginger
  Schmaltz
Yuzu-Koshō
  Schmaltz
Black Pepper
  Bacon Grease

RAMEN
Old-School Shōyu
Old-School Shio

Makes ≈2.4 litres (81 fl oz)
Total cook time: 6 hours

1 kg (2 lb 4 oz) chicken frames
500 g (1 lb 2 oz) chicken wings
100 g (3.5 oz) chicken feet (optional)
1 trotter, split
2 racks (1.2–1.5 kg/2 lb 11 oz–3 lb 5 oz) pork ribs or neck bones
1 onion, skin on, quartered
50 g (1.75 oz) fresh ginger root, thinly sliced
40 g (1.4 oz) niboshi (dried sardines, optional)
20 g (0.7 oz) kombu
10 g (0.35 oz) dried shiitake
≈3.5 litres (118 fl oz) water
20 g (0.7 oz) katsuobushi

Preheat the oven to 200°C fan (425°F). Cook the bones and the fresh vegetables in a deep roasting tray for 45 minutes, turning everything halfway through so that they brown evenly. Use tongs to retrieve the bones and vegetables and place them into a stockpot along with the niboshi (if using), kombu, shiitake and the water (enough to cover). Bring to the lowest possible simmer – between 85–90°C (185–194°F), with no bubbling – then keep cooking at that temperature for 6 hours, skimming the surface often to remove excess fat and scum (keep the fat). Remove from the heat, then add the katsuobushi and leave to infuse for 1 hour. Strain, chill and store according to the guide on page 26, removing any fat that collects at the top of the broth. When decanting the broth, leave behind any cloudy dregs that have settled at the bottom of the container.

スープ

豚骨と鶏ガラ白湯スープ

Tonkotsu to Torigara Paitan Sūpu

Pork and Chicken Paitan

This is a lovely, versatile paitan if you want a little bit of that tonkotsu stink, rounded out with the chickeny fragrance of chicken. It is particularly good in bowls where some lip-licking creaminess is required but not as much as a full-on tonkotsu, such as miso ramen, curry ramen or tantanmen.

TARE
Basic Shio
Shōyu-Shio
 Hybrid
Curry

NOODLES
Toasted Sesame
Springy-Chewy
Egg

OILS
Garlic Sesame
Yuzu-Koshō
 Schmaltz

RAMEN
Tsukemen
Miso
Tantanmen

Makes ≈2.4 litres (81 fl oz)
Total cook time: 8 hours

500 g (1 lb 2 oz) pork femur bones, split
1 kg (2 lb 4 oz) (roughly 2 medium) trotters, split
1 pig's tail
500 g (1 lb 2 oz) (about 2) chicken frames
250 g (8.8 oz) chicken wings
100 g (3.5 oz) chicken feet
200 g (7 oz) chicken skin
≈4 litres (135 fl oz) water, plus extra for blanching
1 leek, coarsely chopped
½ fennel bulb or 2 celery stalks, coarsely chopped
30 g (1 oz) fresh ginger root, thinly sliced
5 garlic cloves
1 star anise
1 bay leaf
½ teaspoon white pepper

Blanch and wash the bones and skin according to the instructions on *page 25*, but remember to remove the chicken from the water shortly after it boils, while leaving the pork to simmer a while longer, as they will take more time to cook than the chicken. Return all of the pork bones (not the chicken bones) to the pot, then add the water (enough to cover). With a lid on the pot, bring to a rolling boil and boil for 2 hours, stirring occasionally. Add the chicken and continue boiling for another 4 hours, topping up the water and stirring frequently. Add all of the vegetables and aromatics and continue to boil for 2 more hours. During this time, allow the broth to reduce (i.e. stop topping up the water). Remove from the heat, then strain, chill and store according to the guide on page 26, or bring back to a simmer if using immediately. Remember to re-emulsify the broth with an immersion blender before serving.

NOTE
The chicken parts here, including the feet, are roughly equivalent to two medium-sized chickens, but you will need to get extra skin from your butcher (or save it from previous chickens).

野菜白湯スープ
Yasai Paitan Sūpu

Vegetable Paitan

Vegetarian paitan is perhaps the most challenging broth to make, or at least, it's been the hardest for me to work out a recipe for. While many vegetarian paitan use soy milk as a base, I find the flavour and mouthfeel of these broths to be, well, too soy milky. Actual vegetables give the broth a fuller, sweeter, more complex flavour. They can be used to thicken the broth, too, by simply blending them up once they're soft. However, the real difficulty in making them is replicating the stickiness of a gelatine-rich broth. To try and achieve this, I have added okra and nattō to the mix.

TARE
Any shio
Miso

NOODLES
Go-To
Hard and Thin
Toasted Sesame

OILS
Black Māyu

RAMEN
Garlic Tonkotsu
Double Soup
Tantanmen

Makes ≈2.1 litres (71 fl oz)
Total boiling time: 60 minutes

1 medium (100 g/3.5 oz) onion, peeled and quartered
½ small fennel bulb (80–100 g/ 2.8–3.5 oz), white part only, quartered
100 g (3.5 oz) hispi cabbage (you can use the core for this)
10 g (0.35 oz) dried shiitake mushrooms
100 g (3.5 oz) shortening
50 g (1.75 oz) waxy potato (peeled weight), diced
≈3 litres (102 fl oz) water
30 garlic cloves, peeled
40 g (1.4 oz) okra
¼ teaspoon white pepper
4 tablespoons nutritional yeast flakes
20 g (0.7 oz) nattō
20 g (0.7 oz) kombu
10 g (0.35 oz) fresh ginger root, peeled and thinly sliced

Combine the onion, fennel, cabbage, shiitake, shortening, potato and water in a stock pot and bring to the boil. Boil with a lid on the pan for 30 minutes, then add the garlic, okra, pepper and yeast flakes. Continue to boil for another 30 minutes, then remove from the heat, take out the shiitake, add the nattō and blend thoroughly with a stick blender. Add the kombu and ginger and leave to steep for 1 hour, then remove the kombu and ginger and pass the broth through a fine sieve. If the yield is significantly less than 2.1 litres (71 fl oz), top it up with water until it reaches this amount; otherwise, the broth will be too thick. Chill and store according to the guide on page 26.

野菜清湯スープ
Yasai Chintan Sūpu

Vegetable Chintan

Vegetable broths are untraditional and remain rare in Japan, but more and more shops abroad are now offering vegetable ramen as more people turn to a plant-based diet. Vegetables are delicious, and because they have no blood and very little fat or protein, it's easy to make a clear broth with good umami and aroma from them. This recipe has a remarkably Bovril-like character. However, because they have no gelatine veg broths tend to lack body. To make up for this, I add a tiny bit of cornflour (cornstarch) to thicken it up, allowing it to coat noodles and toppings better and giving it a silkier mouthfeel.

TARE
Any

NOODLES
Wholegrain
 Jirō-Style
Soba-Ramen
 Hybrid

OILS
Garlic Sesame
Nori
Black Pepper
 Bacon Grease

RAMEN
Miso
Old-School
 Shōyu

Makes ≈2.1 litres (71 fl oz)
Total cook time:
1 hour 30 minutes

1 garlic bulb, halved
250 g (8.8 oz) onion, skin on, thinly sliced
1 small fennel bulb (150–200 g / 5.3–7 oz), thinly sliced
80 g (2.8 oz) button mushrooms, quartered
100 g (3.5 oz) hispi (pointed) cabbage leaves, roughly chopped
150 g (5.3 oz) carrot, cut into 1 cm (½ in) chunks
30 g (1 oz) fresh ginger root, thinly sliced
15 g (0.5 oz) kombu, cut into strips about 2.5 cm (1 in) wide
10 g (0.35 oz) dried shiitake mushrooms
2 tablespoons nutritional yeast flakes
≈3 litres (102 fl oz) water
1 tablespoon cornflour (cornstarch)

Preheat the oven to 200°C fan (425°F). Roast all the veg, including the kombu and shiitake, on a foil-lined baking tray for 20 minutes. This is partly to get a little bit of colour on everything, but mostly to cook out any harsh, raw veg flavour. Tip everything into a stock pot along with the yeast flakes and water, then bring to a bare simmer and hold between 85–90°C (185–194°F) for 1 hour 30 minutes. Pass the broth through a sieve, then let the liquid settle for at least 30 minutes; during this time, any bits of veg that might cloud the broth will settle to the bottom of the container. Slowly pour the liquid back into the (rinsed-out) pot, being careful not to churn up the sediment on the bottom. Leave this sediment behind and discard.

Take a little bit (100 ml-ish/3.5 fl oz) of the broth and stir it together with the cornflour to form a thin slurry, then stir this into the broth and bring to a low boil. Simmer for a few minutes until the mixture thickens. (It won't be very thick, but you'll be able to tell it's more viscous from how the bubbles move through the broth as it simmers.) Pass through a sieve once again, chill and store according to the guide on page 26.

伝統的な鰹出汁
Dentōteki na Katsuo Dashi

Classic Dashi

Dashi on its own is too thin to make ramen broth, but it can't be beaten for delivering umami and a distinct 'Japanese' flavour. If you do want a pure, clean dashi flavour in your ramen, you can use it as is, thickened with a bit of starch to add body.

TARE
Any shio
Bottled mentsuyu/
 shirodashi

NOODLES
Egg
Soba-Ramen Hybrid

OILS
Schmaltz
Allium and Ginger
 Schmaltz
Nori

RAMEN
Old-School Shio
Double Soup

Makes ≈1 litre (34 fl oz)
Total infusion time:
≈1 hour 30 minutes

20 g (0.7 oz) kombu
3–4 dried shiitake mushrooms (optional)
1.2 litres (40 fl oz) water
30 g (1 oz) katsuobushi

Add the kombu and mushrooms (if using) to a saucepan and pour in the water. Set the pan over a very low heat – kombu releases its flavour most readily at a temperature range from cold to about 80°C (175°F). The more time you keep it in that range, the more flavourful your dashi will be. When the water barely begins to simmer, with just a few small bubbles breaking the surface of the water, add the katsuobushi, remove from the heat and leave to infuse for an hour. Pass through a fine sieve, pressing down firmly on the ingredients to extract as much liquid as possible. Dashi will keep in the refrigerator for about a week, but the aroma dissipates quickly, so it's best to use it within a few days.

アサリ鰹出汁
Asari Katsuo Dashi

Clam-Katsuo Dashi

Though shellfish are rarely the star of the show in ramen, they're often part of the chorus. One of the most efficient ways to introduce a strong shellfish flavour to ramen is to simply capture the juice that comes out of clams, which is so delicious it hardly needs seasoning and makes a highly effective dashi. However, like all dashi, it has almost no body; try it in a double soup (*page 182*) where the animal stock can provide gelatine.

TARE
Any shio
Shōyu-Shio Hybrid

NOODLES
Go-To
Soba-Ramen
 Hybrid

OILS
Nori

RAMEN
Old-School Shio
Double Soup

Makes ≈2.1 litres (71 fl oz)
Total infusion time: ≈60 minutes

500 ml (17 fl oz) sake
1 kg (2 lb 4 oz) clams, cleaned
2 litres (68 fl oz) water
50 g (1.75 oz) kombu
60 g (2 oz) katsuobushi

Heat the sake to a simmer in a pot over a high heat. Add the clams and cook until they open, then add the water and kombu. Reduce the heat to low and slowly bring to a bare simmer, then remove from the heat and add the katsuobushi. Leave to infuse for at least half an hour, then pass through a fine sieve. Chill and store according to the guide on page 26.

簡単な魚介類スープ
Kantan na Gyokairui Sūpu

Simple Seafood Broth

Making broth from fish bones has some advantages. Because the bones are so small, they infuse very quickly. Plus, fish bones are comparatively easy to source. However, fish broth doesn't develop the same gelatine content as chicken or pork broths – a good thing if you are planning to use your fish stock as part of a double soup (*page 182*), but if you do want pure fish stock with a bit more body, you can add gelatine directly. Just be mindful of dietary requirements, as most gelatine is not pescetarian-friendly.

TARE
Any shio
Bottled
 mentsuyu/
 shirodashi

NOODLES
Go-To
Springy-Chewy
Soba-Ramen
 Hybrid

OILS
Nori
Black Pepper
 Bacon Grease

RAMEN
Old-School Shio
Double Soup

Makes ≈1 litre (34 fl oz)
Total cook and infusion time:
≈2 hours

200 g (7 oz) fish bones, heads, etc.
100 g (3.5 oz) leek
20 g (0.7 oz) niboshi
20 g (0.7 oz) prawn (shrimp) shells or dried baby prawns
2 ¥500 coin-sized pieces of ginger
1.2 litres (40 fl oz) water
100 ml (3.5 fl oz) dry vermouth or sake
10 g (0.35 oz) kombu
4 leaves gelatine

Combine everything except the kombu and gelatine in a pot and bring to a high simmer. Keep at a high simmer for 30 minutes–1 hour depending on how big the bones are (for just spine and rib bones, a shorter boil is fine; for heads or collars, boil a bit longer). Meanwhile, soak the gelatine in enough cold water to cover. When the broth is done cooking and tastes satisfactorily fishy, stir in the gelatine and add the kombu. Leave to infuse for 1 hour, then pass through a fine sieve, chill and store according to the guide on page 26.

椎茸出汁
Shiitake Dashi

Mushroom Dashi

This is a very simple but effective vegan broth. It has a deep, almost meaty flavour, but it's naturally light on the palate. Like the Vegetable Chintan (*page 37*), this recipe calls for a little cornflour (cornstarch) added at the end to make up for a lack of gelatine, but you can leave it out if you wish – there's a lot of kombu in here, and that provides some body as well.

TARE
Any shio or shōyu
Bottled mentsuyu/
 shirodashi

NOODLES
Springy-Chewy
Soba-Ramen Hybrid

OILS
Garlic Sesame
Nori
Mock Seasoned
 Back Fat

RAMEN
Full English
 Tantanmen
Pizza
Ponzu Reimen

Makes ≈2.1 litres (71 fl oz)
Total infusion time: 2 hours

50 g (1.75 oz) kombu
50 g (1.75 oz) dried shiitake mushrooms
25 g (0.9 oz) dried porcini or similar wild mushrooms
2.5 litres (85 fl oz) water
1 tablespoon cornflour (cornstarch)

Add everything except the cornflour in a pot, and place a drop-lid (see note) directly on top of the ingredients to keep them submerged in the liquid. Set over a low heat, and slowly bring the water to a bare simmer. Once a few small bubbles appear in the water, switch off the heat and leave to infuse for an hour, then pass through a sieve. When decanting, leave behind any dregs that have settled on the bottom of the container.

To increase the viscosity of the dashi, take about 100 ml (3.5 fl oz) of the liquid and stir it together with the cornflour to form a thin slurry. Stir this into the dashi and bring to a low boil. Simmer for a few minutes until the mixture thickens. Chill and store according to the guide on page 26.

NOTE
A drop-lid, or *otoshibuta*, is simply a lid which is slightly too small for the pan it's in, so it rests directly on top of the food. Use one here to keep the shiitake mushrooms from floating to the surface and ensure maximum contact with the water.

Vegetable Jirō-Style Broth

In truth, it is virtually impossible to faithfully make a vegan Jirō-style broth, because the real deal is so pork-forward. However, you can reproduce some of its characteristics, such as its cloudy yet un-emulsified appearance, its meaty umami and its slick mouthfeel. Also, as there's so much going on in a bowl of Jirō, fudging the broth doesn't necessarily weaken the overall impact of the dish, which is to say: Jirō made with this broth will still give you a tummy ache.

TARE
Jirō-Style

NOODLES
Wholegrain
 Jirō-Style

OILS
Garlic Sesame
Nori
Mock Seasoned
 Back Fat

RAMEN
Veganised
 Jirō-Style

Makes ≈1.5 litres (51 fl oz)
Total cook time: 1 hour

50 g (1.75 oz) shortening
100 g (3.5 oz) fresh ginger root, roughly chopped
3 onions, roughly chopped
5 garlic bulbs
50 g (1.75 oz) kombu
50 g (1.75 oz) dried shiitake mushrooms
25 g (0.9 oz) dried porcini
500 ml (17 fl oz) soy milk
≈2 litres (68 fl oz) water
1 tablespoon sesame oil
1 tablespoon cornflour (cornstarch)

Preheat an oven to 200°C fan (425°F). Melt the shortening in a roasting tray in the oven. Once the shortening is hot, tip in all the fresh vegetables (not the dried ones) and toss through the fat, then return to the oven to roast for 20 minutes until nicely coloured. Transfer everything to a stock pot and add everything else except the sesame oil and cornflour. Bring to a high simmer and cook for 1 hour, then remove from the heat. Pass everything through a fine sieve, then return to the (rinsed-out) pan. Mix the cornflour with a little bit of water, then drizzle this mixture into the broth along with the sesame oil, and bring to a high simmer to thicken. Chill and store according to the guide on page 26.

NOTE
The soy milk will split and curdle during the boil. That's good – Jirō-style broth has a cloudy-but-not-creamy look to it. Embrace the curdle.

Other Broth Ideas

Apart from the above, there are many other proteiny items that taste good on ramen. Here are some of my favourites:

Niban Paitan
二番白湯

The first infusion of dashi is called *ichiban* (number one) dashi, and that's the primo stuff – clear and refined, with a strong umami foundation and well-articulated aroma. But there's still flavour left in the base ingredients after this initial extraction, which can be drawn out through a second, more aggressive infusion, resulting in what's known as *niban* (number two) dashi. Similarly, when you make a chintan you extract quite a lot of flavour, but because the water never boils you don't end up breaking down the bones completely, and there's still flavour locked within them. Boiling these spent bones hard for 4–5 hours results in a surprisingly tasty broth. It won't have the rich creaminess usually associated with paitan, so it's a good idea to have this with plenty of schmaltz or lard to reinstate some of the missing mouthfeel and aroma. Although it will be a bit thin, it's still a good utilitarian broth that takes well to richer seasonings and can also be used to dial back paitan that might be too rich.

Microwaved Leftover Roast Chicken Chintan
残り物を使ってレンジで作る鶏清湯

I first learned about making broth in the microwave from an Instagram post by the microwave cookware company Anyday. Though I am a huge advocate for microwave cooking, I didn't think it would be very good for creating gelatine, which only happens with sustained high temperatures or high pressure. I was right – I tried this method, and the resulting broth was quite thin. However, it was tasty and had a sort of 'freshness' you don't get from long-simmered broths. I know microwave cooking has a way of preserving volatile aroma compounds that tend to get lost or destroyed by other cooking methods, so it made sense. The microwave was also very good at rendering fat, and I got a good amount of chīyu (chicken fat) out of just the leaner parts of the bird. It isn't as good as, say, the proper chicken chintan on page 32, but for something you can make in 20 minutes, I'm not complaining.

To make it, combine the remnants of a roast chicken dinner along with whatever aromatics you might want to use in a large microwave-safe bowl and cover loosely with a lid or cling film (plastic wrap). Microwave on high (for me this is 800W) for 10 minutes. Carefully remove the bowl from the microwave and give everything a stir, then re-cover, return to the microwave and cook for another 10 minutes.

スープ

2

TARE

Broth, just like any food, needs seasoning – lots of it. That's where our friend tare comes in. If you're making broth at home, you don't strictly need to make tare – you can just season it directly with salt, soy sauce, miso or other salty, umami-rich ingredients. However, tare adds another dimension of flavour to broths, and it makes ramen more customisable. Tare is essential for a professional ramen set-up because it allows for control over the consistency of the seasoning, and it also enables a shop to sell multiple types of ramen with just one broth.

First and foremost, tare should add salt to the bowl, which will underscore the broth's natural umami and snap its flavours into focus. But tare should also bring its own umami to the party. The most direct and easy way to do this is by adding monosodium glutamate, but there are other umami compounds – inosinate and guanylate – that amplify glutamate in an effect called 'synergistic umami', which simply means that their impact is more than the sum of their parts when used in conjunction with one another. Glutamate is readily extracted from a wide variety of things, especially kombu, while inosinate and guanylate are a bit less common. The former is typically derived from dried or preserved fish, while the latter can be easily extracted from dried mushrooms.

In Japan, the pure salts of these compounds are sold under various brand names, such as Ajinomoto's Haimī, but as far as I'm aware these are not available outside of Japan. However, they can be found in Japanese dashi and chicken stock powders, which will put you in the fast lane to Umami Town. Just look for the ingredient 'disodium 5'-ribonucleotides' or the E number 635 on the label to make sure you're getting the good stuff.

There are three main categories of tare: shio (salt), shōyu (soy sauce) and miso. But just like chintan and paitan, these categories are not as cut-and-dry as they seem. Many tare are actually a blend of two or three of these seasonings, but to keep things simple, I have designated each of the recipes here as one of the three.

HOW TO TARE
タレの使い方
TARE NO TSUKAIKATA

TARE STORAGE
タレの保存方法
TARE NO HOZON HŌHŌ

Most tare are in the ballpark of 10–15% salt, which means every 10 ml (2 teaspoons) has about 1–1.5 g (0.03–0.05 oz) salt. Most ramen ought to have about 3–6 g (0.1–0.2 oz) salt per bowl, so that's anywhere from 20–60 ml (0.7–2 fl oz) tare. These are broad generalisations, of course, and both the tare and the dosage can vary widely, especially when accounting for individual tastes. But these numbers are good to bear in mind when making your own tare; in fact, you can tare-ify any liquid – such as a broth – by adding 10–15 g (0.35–0.5 oz) salt for every 100 ml (3.5 fl oz). Add some MSG and you'll have a damn good tare there, even if the liquid is just water. Conveniently, the salt content of most soy sauces and many types of miso falls within this range, which means that in a pinch, they make reliably tasty tare on their own.

Most tare can just be dosed into the bottom of each bowl before adding the hot broth, but there are a few exceptions to flag. The first one is miso, which needs whisking or blending to incorporate; it's also common for miso tare to be boiled into the soup. The others to note are the tantan tare and curry tare, which are 'secondary' tare. This means that they add a particular flavour but not salt, so they need to be used in conjunction with another base tare to season the bowl. They are also thick, so they need to be whisked or blended just like miso tare. In the case of curry tare, it should be boiled in broth for at least 5 minutes in order to cook out the spices.

You can use any tare with any broth, of course, but consider how you want the flavours to come together. Some broths that are more delicately flavoured will be obliterated by a strong miso or shōyu tare, while some rich, funky broths benefit from them. Before you go all-in with a particular tare and broth combination, try a little bit first. Then you can adjust the tare accordingly (with more or less salt or aromatic ingredients) or go back to the drawing board and try something entirely different.

Kept in the refrigerator, tare last for a very long time because of their high salt content – months rather than weeks. However, flavours start to fade after a while, and a tinge of sourness can creep into tare that have been around for too long. I think it is best to use tare within a month.

タレ

基本的な塩タレ
Kantan na Shio Tare

Basic Shio Tare

I call this 'basic', although really the most basic shio tare would be something along the lines of just water and salt, maybe with a sheet of kombu and/or some MSG thrown in for umami. This tare recipe is still mostly straight-up salt and MSG, but with added fragrance and synergistic umami from sake, shiitake mushrooms and kombu. The chicken powder and dashi powder are used primarily for the umami compounds they contain, but they will also add a subtle flavour to the soup – go with chicken for, you know, a more chickeny (and slightly garlicky-gingery) flavour, dashi for a delicate fishy smokiness, or you can opt for a little of both.

BROTHS
Any

RAMEN
Garlic Tonkotsu
Old-School Shio
Tantanmen

Makes 450 ml (15 fl oz)
Dose per 300 ml (10 fl oz) broth:
≈30–50 ml (1–1.7 fl oz)

350 ml (11.8 fl oz) water
150 ml (5 fl oz) sake
4–6 g (0.15–0.2 oz) (about 1 large) dried shiitake mushroom
5 g (0.2 oz) kombu
50 g (1.75 oz) salt
20 g (0.7 oz) MSG
1 tablespoon chicken powder and/or katsuo dashi powder
1 teaspoon sugar

Combine the water, sake, shiitake and kombu in a saucepan and leave at room temperature for 1 hour. Set over a low heat and gradually bring the liquid to a very, very low simmer – it should be steaming, with just a few small bubbles breaking the surface. Switch off the heat and leave to infuse for another hour, turning over the mushroom to make sure it fully infuses. Pass this mixture though a fine sieve, then stir in the remaining ingredients until they fully dissolve.

即席塩タレ
Sokuseki Shio Tare

Quick Shio Tare

This is essentially a rough-and-ready, very speedy version of the basic shio recipe above, which you can make in just a few minutes. Additional stock powder makes up for the umami compounds that would have otherwise come from shiitake mushrooms and kombu, and they work splendidly.

BROTHS
Any

RAMEN
Garlic Tonkotsu
Old-School Shio
Tantanmen

Makes 450 ml (15 fl oz)
Dose per 300 ml (10 fl oz) broth:
≈30–50 ml (1–1.7 fl oz)

400 ml (14 fl oz) water
50 ml (1.7 fl oz) sake
50 g (1.75 oz) salt
20 g (0.7 oz) MSG
2 tablespoons chicken powder and/or dashi powder
2 teaspoons sugar

Combine everything in a jar and shake it up until the powders dissolve.

煮干しタレ
Niboshi Tare

Niboshi Tare

Niboshi (dried sardines) are a key ingredient in many styles of ramen, with a distinctive flavour – obviously quite fishy, but in a lighter, fresher way than the deep, rich smokiness of katsuobushi. This niboshi-forward tare allows you to add that particular old-school sardine flavour to any bowl you like.

BROTHS
Any

RAMEN
Old-School Shōyu
Old-School Shio
Double Soup

Makes 400 ml (14 fl oz)
Dose per 300 ml (10 fl oz) broth:
≈30–50 ml (1–1.7 fl oz)

10 g (0.35 oz) kombu
20 g (0.7 oz) niboshi
450 ml (15 fl oz) water
2 tablespoons shōyu
2 tablespoons usukuchi soy sauce
35 g (1.25 oz) salt
10 g (0.35 oz) MSG

Combine the kombu, niboshi and water in a container and keep in the refrigerator for a few hours or overnight. Transfer to a saucepan and slowly bring to a bare simmer over a low heat. When the water starts to bubble, remove the kombu and continue to heat the niboshi until it comes to a low boil. Boil for 5 minutes, then remove from the heat, pass through a sieve and stir in the remaining ingredients.

スタウトとトマトの醬油タレ
Sutauto to Tomato no Shōyu Tare

Stout and Tomato Shōyu Tare

This is based on the main shōyu tare we used at the restaurant for years. The thinking behind it is that stout and tomato carry the tang and rich umami of soy sauce, while balancing its salinity. This makes it a great tare if you want a shōyu-forward bowl and it's also perfect for poaching chicken for chāshū (page 120).

BROTHS
Chicken Paitan
Pork and Chicken
 Paitan
Roast Pork and
 Chicken Chintan
Vegetable Chintan
Mushroom Dashi

RAMEN
Curry
Tantanmen
Full English
 Tantanmen
Pizza
Half a Pig's Head
Leftover Nando's

Makes 300 ml (10 fl oz)
Dose per 300 ml (10 fl oz) broth:
≈30–50 ml (1–1.7 fl oz)

300 ml (10 fl oz) shōyu
1 star anise
12 g (0.4 oz) (about 2–3) dried shiitake mushrooms
100 ml (3.5 fl oz) stout (don't use anything too bitter or too thin; Guinness Export is a good example of what you're after)
30 g (1 oz) tomato paste (purée)
10 g (0.35 oz) kombu

Combine everything except the kombu in a saucepan and slowly bring to a high simmer over a low heat. Simmer for 5 minutes, then remove from the heat. Leave to cool for 10 minutes and then add the kombu. Leave to infuse at room temperature for 2 hours, then pass everything through a sieve, pressing down hard on the solids with the back of a ladle to extract as much liquid as possible.

52

タレ

二郎系タレ
Jirō-kei Tare

Jirō-Style Tare

When I was first researching Jirō-style ramen some years ago, I read that the tare was two parts soy sauce to one part MSG. Now there's a tare that takes no prisoners. But I did some more research while trying to make a vegan Jirō – mostly informed by Elvin Yung's (@shikaku.ramen) incredibly detailed article on the subject – and ultimately settled on this recipe. It's suitably punchy and un-subtle for use in Jirō-style bowls, but it works with other styles as well, especially ones where nuance is not a priority.

BROTHS
Jirō-Style
Mushroom Dashi

RAMEN
Jirō-Style
Tantanmen
Curry

Makes 60 ml (2 fl oz), 1 serving
Dose per 350 ml (11.8 fl oz) broth:
60 ml (2 fl oz)

2 tablespoons shōyu
1 tablespoon usukuchi soy sauce
1 tablespoon mirin
½ teaspoon MSG

Combine everything in the bowl as you make the ramen.

NOTE
This tare is so simple it can just be whacked into each bowl as you assemble the ramen, but if you like, you can scale it up and keep it in larger batches. Simply stir everything together until the MSG dissolves.

基本的な醤油タレ
Kihonteki na Shōyu Tare

Basic Shōyu Tare

This is a simple shōyu tare, only slightly more complicated than adding straight soy sauce to your bowl. Blending three soy sauces together provides a balanced, interesting flavour, while the use of shiitake mushrooms and katsuobushi adds important umami compounds and some aroma as well.

BROTHS
Any

RAMEN
Old-School Shōyu
Curry
Tokyo Modern

Makes 450 ml (15 fl oz)
Dose per 300 ml (10 fl oz) broth:
≈45–60 ml (1.5–2 fl oz)

8 g (0.3 oz) dried shiitake mushrooms (about 1 large or 2 small)
100 ml (3.5 fl oz) water
75 ml (2.5 fl oz) mirin
50 ml (1.7 fl oz) sake
5 g (0.2 oz) katsuobushi
200 ml (6.75 fl oz) shōyu
150 ml (5 fl oz) usukuchi soy sauce
50 ml (1.7 fl oz) tamari

Using a serrated knife or strong kitchen shears, cut the shiitake into small pieces so they infuse more quickly and evenly. Combine the cut-up shiitake with the water, mirin and sake in a saucepan and leave at room temperature for 2–4 hours. Bring the liquid to a high simmer, then add the katsuobushi. Simmer for 5 minutes, then remove from the heat and leave to infuse for another hour. Pass through a sieve, pressing down hard on the ingredients to extract as much liquid as possible. Combine this liquid with the soy sauces and mix.

即席和風醤油タレ
Sokuseki Wafū Shōyu Tare

Quick Wafū Shōyu Tare

This is a mentsuyu-inspired soy sauce tare you can bash together quickly using dashi powder as a shortcut, delivering a rounded umami profile and subtle katsuobushi flavour without the need for lengthy infusions. It's not quite as good as a 'real' katsuo tare, but it works perfectly well in ramen where the tare is not the star of the show anyway.

BROTHS
Any

RAMEN
Old-School Shōyu
Double Soup

Makes 450 ml (15 fl oz)
Dose per 300 ml (10 fl oz) broth:
≈45–60 ml (1.5–2 fl oz)

50 ml (1.7 fl oz) sake

25 ml (1 tablespoon
plus 2 teaspoons) mirin

25 ml (1 tablespoon
plus 2 teaspoons) water

5 g (0.2 oz) salt

1 tablespoon brown sugar

20 g (0.7 oz) dashi powder

150 ml (5 fl oz) shōyu

50 ml (1.7 fl oz) usukuchi soy sauce

50 ml (1.7 fl oz) tamari

Stir the sake, mirin, water, salt, brown sugar and dashi powder together until everything dissolves. Add the soy sauces and mix well.

KEY POINT

Using good-quality soy sauces makes a huge difference, and I would recommend seeking out at least one unpasteurised (nama) soy sauce for this. It will make your ramen taste fresher and more aromatic, with subtle fruity-malty notes.

醤油と塩の合わせタレ

Shōyu to Shio no Awase Tare

Shōyu-Shio Hybrid Tare

Shōyu tare is delicious, but it can be overpowering, especially in lighter chintan broths. This version uses just a little bit of shōyu in conjunction with salt to provide a rich, tangy flavour without obscuring the subtleties of your broth.

BROTHS
Any

RAMEN
Garlic Tonkotsu
Old-School Shōyu
Double Soup

Makes 350 ml (11.8 fl oz)
Dose per 300 ml (10 fl oz) broth:
≈30–50 ml (1–1.7 fl oz)

5 g (0.2 oz) kombu
1 sheet nori
1 small-ish (3 g/0.1 oz) dried shiitake mushroom
250 ml (8.5 fl oz) sake
100 ml (3.5 fl oz) water
75 ml (2.5 fl oz) mirin
30 g (1 oz) salt
10 g (0.35 oz) MSG
50 ml (1.7 fl oz) shōyu
50 ml (1.7 fl oz) usukuchi soy sauce
10 ml (2 teaspoons) fish sauce

Combine the kombu, nori, shiitake, sake, water and mirin in a saucepan and leave to infuse for 1 hour. Bring to a bare simmer, then remove from the heat. Leave to infuse for another hour, then pass through a sieve and add all the remaining ingredients, stirring so the salt and MSG dissolve.

フルーティで
ニンニク風味の味噌タレ
Furūti de Ninniku Fūmi no Miso Tare

Fruity-Garlicky Miso Tare

 One of my favourite bowls of miso ramen comes from the Sapporo institution Sumire, which uses a delicious tare with prominent notes of fruity miso and heady garlic. I did some research but ultimately failed to find Sumire's actual tare recipe. However, I did get some ideas along the way for how to create a similar aroma, somehow both simple and complex, fruity, fresh, sweet and musky all at once.

BROTHS
Any paitan

RAMEN
Miso
Pizza
Wisconsin Beer
and Cheese

Makes 400 g/320 ml (10.8 fl oz)
Dose per 300 ml (10 fl oz):
≈60–80 g/45–60 ml (1.5–2 fl oz)

100 g (3.5 oz) red miso
50 g (1.75 oz) moromi miso
150 g (5.3 oz) unpasteurised white miso
2 tablespoons lard
12 garlic cloves, coarsely chopped
15 g (0.5 oz) fresh ginger root, peeled and finely chopped
1 tablespoon ground coriander
1 teaspoon garlic granules
½ teaspoon *gochugaru* (Korean chilli (hot pepper) flakes), Aleppo pepper or similar fruity chilli flakes
6 tablespoons fruity white wine (nothing too dry or acidic)
4 tablespoons mirin
1 tablespoon light brown sugar
2 tablespoons olive oil
1 tablespoon sesame oil
5 g (0.2 oz) salt

Stir together the miso until well mixed. Heat the lard in a small saucepan over a medium-low heat, then add all but 2 garlic cloves. Sauté for about 10 minutes, stirring often, until it softens and browns. Add the ginger and continue to cook for about 2–3 minutes to soften, then add about a quarter of the miso mixture and the dry spices and sauté for 2–3 minutes so they infuse into the fat. Add the wine and mirin and boil for 3–4 minutes to cook off the alcohol and reduce slightly, then remove from the heat and add the sugar, olive oil and sesame oil. Leave to cool for a few minutes, then whisk in the remaining miso, garlic and the salt. Transfer everything to a food processor or blender and blitz until smooth.

タレ

味噌タレ
Miso Tare

Miso Tare

I have always loved miso ramen but never really made a good one until I read self-described 'Sapporo ramen nerd' Mike Satinover's recipe for miso tare, which is a lot more complex than mine ever was – 14 ingredients compared to my four. The results speak for themselves, and this recipe is very much indebted to his. The additions of cream, cheese and malt are informed by a few recipes in *Ramen Taizen*, which I have included partly for a subtle sweetness, but more as a reference to Hokkaido's history of dairy farming and brewing.

BROTHS
Any paitan
Roast Pork and
  Chicken Chintan

RAMEN
Miso
Pizza
Curry

Makes 400 g/320 ml (10.8 fl oz)
Dose per 300 ml (10 fl oz):
≈60–80 g/45–60 ml (1.5–2 fl oz)

150 g (5.3 oz) red miso
100 g (3.5 oz) white miso
50 g (1.75 oz) Hatchō or brown rice miso
2 tablespoons vegetable oil or animal fat
1 onion, finely chopped
4 garlic cloves, finely chopped
20 g (0.7 oz) fresh ginger root, peeled and finely chopped
6 tablespoons sake
1 tablespoon sesame oil
1 tablespoon sesame seeds, crushed
4 tablespoons single (light) cream
4 tablespoons Ovaltine or malt powder
30 g (1 oz) Parmesan or mature Cheddar, finely grated
1 tablespoon shōyu

Stir together the three types of miso until well mixed. Heat the oil or fat in a small saucepan over a medium-high heat, then add the onion, garlic and ginger. Sauté for about 10 minutes, stirring often, until everything softens and begins to colour, then add roughly half of the miso mixture and continue to cook for another 7–8 minutes, until the miso darkens as well. Whisk in the sake and boil for 3–4 minutes to cook off the alcohol, then add the sesame oil, sesame seeds and the cream. Bring to the boil and cook for another 3–4 minutes, stirring often. Remove from the heat, leave to cool for a few minutes, then whisk in the Ovaltine, cheese, shōyu and remaining miso mixture. Transfer everything to a blender or food processor and process until smooth.

Tantan Tare

We began making tantanmen at the restaurant as a Christmas special, with a kind of cute, kind of macabre connection to the holiday: we made it with reindeer meat. For something so gimmicky, it was very tasty and we kept it on the menu, changing it up with the seasons. In spring we used lamb, in summer, courgette (zucchini) and aubergine (eggplant), pigeon in the autumn (fall) and back to reindeer in the winter. We used a very basic sesame and chilli paste as the base, until our chef Sana told me he thought he could make a better version and, sure enough, his was way better. We stuck with it from then on. I have a lot of respect for his command of a good tantan tare, which features roasted peppers and a subtle but spot-on use of spices. This recipe is based on his, so thank you, Sana, wherever you are!

Makes 600 g/500 ml (17 fl oz)
Dose per 300 ml (10 fl oz) bowl:
≈80 g/60 ml (2 fl oz)

300 g (10.6 oz) red (bell) peppers (about 2), deseeded and coarsely chopped
1 small-ish (about 5 g/0.2 oz) Scotch bonnet (keep the seeds in if you want this hot, which is what I'd recommend), de-stemmed and coarsely chopped
6 garlic cloves, peeled but let whole
¼ teaspoon salt
2 tablespoons vegetable oil or animal fat of your choice
1 tablespoon gochugaru (or similar medium-hot chilli (hot pepper) flakes)
1 teaspoon ground cumin
1 teaspoon ground coriander
½ teaspoon ground black pepper
250 g (8.8 oz) sesame paste
juice of ½ lemon (about 1 tablespoon)
60 ml (4 tablespoons) water
2 tablespoons sesame oil
1 tablespoon shōyu

Combine the peppers, Scotch bonnet, garlic, salt and oil in a saucepan and heat over a medium heat with a lid on the pan for about 15 minutes, stirring often, until the peppers and garlic are nicely browned and very soft. (Switch on the extractor and maybe even open a window when you do this, because the vapourised capsaicin from the Scotch bonnet can really irritate your eyes and throat.) Add the dry spices and cook for a few minutes more, stirring well, then add the sesame paste and lemon, stir briefly and remove from the heat. Add the water, sesame oil and shōyu, and blend until totally smooth. Keep in the refrigerator for up to 2 weeks.

NOTE

You can use tahini for this, and it will be adequate, but I recommend going for the Chinese equivalent instead, typically labelled 'sesame sauce'. It has a richer, nuttier flavour than tahini, which will make a big difference to your finished tantanmen.

カレータレ
Karē Tare

Curry Tare

This is a seasoning paste to make curry soup, which can be worked into basically any broth or style of ramen, but I developed it specifically to replicate Muroran curry ramen (page 164), which is my current obsession. This tare only has enough salt to season itself, not the whole bowl, so it needs to be used in conjunction with another tare – miso or shōyu would be my recommendations. This tare also must be boiled into soup in order to fully cook out the spices – so don't just lob it into the bowl.

BROTHS
Pork and Chicken
  Paitan
Niban Paitan
Roast Pork and
  Chicken Chintan

RAMEN
Curry

Makes 500 g/480 ml (16 fl oz)
Dose per 300 ml (10 fl oz):
45–60 ml/g (1.5–2 fl oz)

50 g (1.75 oz) animal fat of your choice
120 g (4.2 oz) onion (1 medium), finely diced
80 g (2.8 oz) sweet potato, peeled and coarsely grated
15 g (0.5 oz) fresh ginger root, peeled and thinly sliced
3 garlic cloves
10 g (0.35 oz) fresh chilli (use whatever chilli you like, deseeded or not, depending on your preference for heat)
150 g (5.3 oz) tomato (1 medium), chopped
4 tablespoons garam masala
2½ tablespoons mild Madras curry powder
1½ tablespoons hot Madras curry powder
1 tablespoon five-spice powder
300 ml (10 fl oz) water
100 g (3.5 oz) tonkatsu sauce
2 tablespoons shōyu
1 teaspoon cornflour (cornstarch)

Melt the fat in a saucepan over a medium heat and add the onion. Cook until evenly browned (about 12–15 minutes), stirring often. Add the sweet potato, ginger, garlic and chilli, and continue to cook for about 5 minutes, stirring frequently, until they begin to colour as well. Add the tomato and spices, and keep cooking for another 5 minutes, stirring constantly to ensure they don't catch on the bottom. Add the water and tonkatsu sauce and simmer for about 10 minutes, then stir together the shōyu and cornflour and pour it into the simmering liquid. Remove from the heat and use a stick blender to process into a smooth purée. Because this is not very salty, it will only keep in the refrigerator for up to a week, but it can be frozen (ice cube trays are handy) for up to 6 months.

To use, add 4 tablespoons of the paste to 300 ml (10 fl oz) of broth in a saucepan and bring to the boil, then cook for about 5 minutes, stirring frequently, then whisk in a miso or shōyu tare, to taste. It is then ready to eat.

タレ

3 NOODLES

You may have seen this quote here and there in ramen circles, mostly deployed as a pithy marketing slogan: 'If you don't make your own noodles, you're just a soup shop.' This is attributed to some ramen master in Japan and I hate it. First of all, 'just a soup shop' is a pretty haughty dismissal of everything that goes into making ramen apart from the noodles. Secondly, making your own noodles doesn't mean your ramen will necessarily be better than anyone else's, just like making your own bread won't necessarily make your sandwiches better. The enormous majority of ramen shops in Japan *don't* make their own noodles, because it's a job better left to dedicated specialists. Making noodles is difficult, and to make any significant quantity requires dangerous, costly machinery. There is little sense in making your own noodles if you run a ramen shop.

HOWEVER. In working on this book and a few other ramen-related projects, I have rediscovered noodle making and found it to be a joyful experience. This is mostly due to gaining a better understanding of the process, but it's also because I only make a few portions at a time, and because I bought a pasta cutting attachment for my KitchenAid, which makes the whole endeavour immeasurably more achievable and enjoyable. In fact, I would issue a huge caveat for this entire chapter: if you are going to attempt to make your own noodles, even only occasionally, you really should invest in some kind of mechanised roller. This isn't just because it's quicker and easier, it's also because ramen dough is so tough and dry it could actually break your machine if it's one of those hand-cranked ones.

THE JOY OF NOODLES
麺の幸甚
MEN NO KŌJIN

Fresh, well-made noodles are a singular delight, so full of verve and fragrance. But the best thing about making your own noodles is that once you understand the basics, you can make them however you want. Even if good noodles are already available to you, it's great fun to try and create your own perfect noodle.

So what is your perfect noodle? It really depends on your ramen. Different soups call for different noodles because of how they interact with each other.

TIPS ON COOKING NOODLES

Cooking noodles is the easy part, but it can still go wrong. Some tips to bear in mind:

- Minimise the recovery time it takes for the water to return to the boil after dropping the noodles in by using a large quantity of water set on your strongest burner and having the noodles at room temperature before cooking.

- Use noodle baskets for easy removal and draining. Ensure you shake off as much excess water from the basket as possible so you don't dilute your soup.

- Use chopsticks to stir the noodles within the baskets as they boil to promote even cooking and reduce the risk of clumping.

- Have everything else ready before cooking the noodles. The temperature of the broth and the texture of the noodles are two of the most important sensory elements of ramen, and both of those things deteriorate quickly after plating, so have all of your mise en place done and laid out ahead of time.

- Noodle cooking times depend on a lot of factors, but the main one is noodle thickness. Thin noodles will only take 30 seconds or perhaps less to boil; thicker ones can be anywhere from a minute to three (or possibly longer). If you're not sure – and you won't be the first time around – check them every 20 seconds by fishing one out with chopsticks and trying it.

PRINCIPLES IN PAIRING NOODLES WITH SOUP
麺とスープの合い方
MEN TO SŪPU NO AIKATA

Noodles ought to act as a conveyor for soup, and this can happen in three ways. One is by allowing the noodles to absorb some of the broth. The second is through capillary action, by drawing up broth in the tiny channels formed in between noodles as they hang parallel to each other when picked up by chopsticks. The third way is simply by having the broth coat the noodles and cling to them.

Which method of soup conveyance you aim for will largely depend on the consistency of your broth, which will then determine what kind of noodles to try. But before we get into specifics, it's a good idea to understand the constituent parts of ramen noodle dough and how they affect the finished product.

1. FLOUR
There are innumerable varieties of flour to choose from for making ramen, but for the purposes of this book and understanding the basics, any off-the-shelf strong white bread flour will do. Bread flours have a high gluten content, which is necessary for developing ramen's characteristic strength. Some recipes call for vital wheat gluten in addition to bread flour to increase that strength even further. Some recipes call for alternative flours for a particular aroma or texture, and these are generally more supple and tender (but this can be counteracted by adding more gluten).

2. WATER
Ramen in general has *very* low hydration – the amount of the water can be anywhere from 22–50% of the weight of the flour, but mostly it falls within the 30–40% range. (This is much lower than, say, pasta dough, which is well over 50%.) Small variations in water content can make a pretty big difference on the outcome of the noodle, so it's important to be precise.

Hydration levels affect noodle texture in a variety of ways, but there are two I think are of key importance. Firstly, the more water you add to the dough, the more it activates gluten formation, which results in a stronger, chewier noodle. The inverse of this is that lower hydration noodles are more snappy and brittle, and also generally straighter. Secondly, higher hydration noodles cook more evenly, which means they tend to have a more uniform texture throughout the noodle. This also helps them absorb more broth.

3. KANSUI
Kansui is what makes ramen ramen, the alkaline minerals that alter the noodle's gluten structure and enhance its chewiness. Basically, more kansui = more toothsome noodles. It also adds a slightly sulphurous 'chemical' aroma, which is particularly noticeable in doughs made with egg. Kansui is made up of potassium carbonate (K_2CO_3) and sodium carbonate (Na_2CO_3), usually more of the latter than the former. Potassium stiffens the dough and makes a harder, more rigid noodle, while sodium makes it more elastic and bouncy. You can buy off-the-shelf kansui mixes, but I get each one individually and blend them using one part potassium to two parts sodium. This makes a good, all-purpose kansui which works well in most noodles.

4. SALT
While salt does affect gluten formation, I tend to think of salt in ramen mainly how I think of it in anything else: as seasoning. And since most of that will come from the soup, you don't need much.

→

5. EGG
Egg has some interesting and useful effects on noodle dough. First of all, whole eggs or egg yolks contribute a rich, golden colour, which is desirable in certain types of noodle. Yolks also add a delicious eggy flavour and make the dough more supple and tender, easier to work with and less tough when cooked. Whites make the dough more brittle and snappy and also more resilient in broth – think of the rubbery texture of a fully cooked egg white. It's firm and breaks cleanly, and doesn't soften when it gets wet. It contributes these characteristics to noodles as well. Using whole egg makes the dough more workable and helps to produce a versatile, middle -of-the-road texture, neither too soft nor too hard, not too snappy nor too chewy.

Understanding these ingredients should help you figure out what sort of texture your noodles will have, and how they'll behave once boiled and dropped into soup. Very generally speaking – there are many exceptions to this – here's what noodles I'd go for depending on the broth:

THINNER SOUPS
Thinner soups, such as chintan or dashi, don't have the viscosity to cling to noodles so it's best to use chewy, curly, more absorbent noodles that allow some of the broth to soak in. There are three primary ways to make noodles more absorbent: by using flours with a lower gluten content, by using more water in the dough and/or by cooking the noodles a bit longer. The latter is probably the most important – this is sort of counter-intuitive to me, but significantly hydrated noodles will soak up more liquid. Think of it this way: if you put dry pasta into a bowl of hot soup, it will basically never soften. But if you put cooked pasta into soup, it will begin to absorb the liquid and soften immediately.

For me, the perfect noodle for thinner soups is one with relatively high hydration (around 37–40%) but also high protein and high kansui content, so that it retains its chew even after soaking up some broth.

THICKER SOUPS
Thicker soups, such as tonkotsu, tantan or curry, can use any noodle, but the classic choice is to use hard, straight, less absorbent noodles which can easily become coated in fat and gelatine and draw it up via capillary action. Because viscous broths have less available water, they don't get absorbed into noodles as readily, so this isn't the best way for them to convey broth. The classic example of this pairing, of course, is in Kyushu-style tonkotsu, which uses extremely low hydration, quickly cooked, hard noodles in a creamy pork broth. However, because broths like these are so thick, they tend to cling to any kind of noodle. Tsukemen, which probably has the thickest form of broth there is, tends to use chunky noodles that can be either wavy or straight. I don't know why this is the norm, but it does make for a very satisfying mouthful, just like thick, doughy pasta in a rich sauce.

The following chart places noodle characteristics on multiple axes, with descriptors of how you might achieve those characteristics listed below.

HARD

COOKED LESS
LOWER HYDRATION
MORE GLUTEN
MORE POTASSIUM CARBONATE
CONTAINS EGG WHITE

TENDER

COOKED MORE
HIGHER HYDRATION
LESS GLUTEN
LESS KANSUI
CONTAINS EGG YOLK
CONTAINS ALTERNATIVE FLOURS

BRITTLE

LOWER HYDRATION
LESS KANSUI
MORE POTASSIUM CARBONATE
CONTAINS EGG WHITE

CHEWY

HIGHER HYDRATION
MORE KANSUI
MORE SODIUM CARBONATE
MORE GLUTEN

RESILIENT

COOKED LESS
LOWER HYDRATION
CONTAINS EGG WHITE

ABSORBENT

COOKED MORE
HIGHER HYDRATION
LESS GLUTEN

STRAIGHT

KEPT STRAIGHT AFTER CUTTING
LOWER HYDRATION
LESS SODIUM CARBONATE

CURLY

TEMOMI APPLIED AFTER CUTTING
HIGHER HYDRATION
MORE SODIUM CARBONATE

NEUTRAL

LOWER HYDRATION
LESS KANSUI
CONTAINS WHITE FLOUR ONLY
LESS RESTED

AROMATIC

HIGHER HYDRATION
MORE KANSUI
CONTAINS EGG
CONTAINS ALTERNATIVE FLOURS
MORE RESTED

麺

MAKING NOODLES
麺の作り方
MEN NO TSUKURIKATA

Once you've decided what noodle to make – make them! But before we do, I should give credit where credit is due. My current noodle-making process and understanding of alkaline noodles generally comes almost entirely from two texts, Mike and Scott Satinover's *The Ramen_Lord Book of Ramen* and Pippa Middlehurst's *Dumplings and Noodles*. Both of these books, especially *Ramen_Lord's*, go into much more detail regarding the science and technique of making noodles, so please do seek them out to improve your skills and fine-tune your noodles even further.

1. COMBINE THE WATER, KANSUI, SALT AND, IF THE RECIPE CALLS FOR IT, FRESH EGG. Use microscales for this. Stir the kansui and salt into the water (cool tap water, not warm) with a little whisk until they dissolve. Kansui has a tendency to clump up, but just keep whisking and it will dissolve eventually. If you're patient, the kansui will dissolve on its own after about 15 minutes; if you're impatient you can use a stick blender. If you are using egg, weigh this and whisk it separately first, then blend it into the kansui-salt water, otherwise it will impede the dissolution of the kansui.

2. COMBINE THE FLOUR(S), WHEAT GLUTEN, POWDERED EGG AND ANY OTHER DRY INGREDIENTS. Simply weigh them out into the bowl of your stand mixer, then use the paddle attachment on the mixer to mix the flours, on the lowest speed, for about a minute.

3. ADD THE WATER MIXTURE TO THE DRY MIXTURE IN A VERY SLOW, STEADY STREAM. Imagine you are making a mayonnaise here: you want to incorporate the water gradually so it hydrates the flour evenly. At this stage I put the mixer on the second-lowest speed, still using the paddle attachment, and very slowly pour in the liquid. Some of the liquid will land on the paddle and create clumps of wetter dough. Once all of the liquid has been added, scrape these clumps off and incorporate them back into the dough by mixing for another minute or so.

It is wise to have an electric pasta roller for this, although a hand-cranked machine will be okay for higher hydration (>36% water) doughs. This method also requires the use of a stand mixer. You can make noodle dough without one, and for this method I would direct you to Hugh Amano and Sarah Becan's *Let's Make Ramen!*, which has a detailed guide to this process. The steps below all assume you are using one of the recipes in this book, all of which are designed to make four portions of ramen.

4. COMPRESS THE CLUMPS.
Correctly made noodle dough looks wrong. What I mean by this is that the dough will not come together cohesively on its own. Upon mixing, it forms little clumps or shreds, but it won't form a solid dough until you apply pressure. Do this by simply squeezing and kneading the dough together until it forms a crumbly mass. It still won't hold together well at this point – but don't worry, it will.

5. FLATTEN THE DOUGH AND REST IT IN A PLASTIC BAG. Transfer your crumbly dough to a large plastic Zip-loc bag. (By 'large' I mean the kind that are about 27 cm (10¾ in) square, which are the perfect size for this.) Spread the dough out within the bag so that it occupies most of the area of the bag in a roughly even layer. Use a rolling pin to firmly press the dough so it squashes together and forms a more consistent depth, as well as a rectangular shape. Seal the bag and leave to rest it for 30 minutes or more. As it rests, the dough will soften, making it easier to roll out. (Full credit to David Chan of @nichijou.ramen for the brilliant Zip-loc bag technique.)

6. REMOVE THE DOUGH FROM THE BAG AND CUT IT INTO FOUR ROUGHLY EQUAL RECTANGLES. They're likely to fall apart a bit. That's okay – they'll come back together as we roll them.

麺 →

7. START FEEDING EACH RECTANGLE OF DOUGH THROUGH THE MACHINE ON ITS WIDEST SETTING. If your dough is much more than an about half a centimetre (¼ in) thick at this point, grab the rolling pin and flatten it a bit more. Feed it through the roller (on the lowest or second-lowest speed if you're using a stand mixer attachment) to begin sheeting. The dough will be crumbly and fragile. It will probably break apart completely. Keep folding and pressing it back together, then feeding it back through the machine and eventually it will start to form relatively smooth, cohesive sheets.

8. FOLD, FLATTEN AND SHAPE THE SHEET. At the beginning of rolling, every time you feed the dough through the roller, you should fold it back onto itself. Always fold it in the same direction, which will strengthen the dough's structure, creating a better bite. Once your dough has formed a relatively smooth, even sheet, you may notice that the sides of the sheet are still raggedy. You can fold

these in towards the centre of the dough to create straighter edges, pressing them down firmly with your fists or a rolling pin before feeding it through the roller again. (But don't worry too much about this – you'll trim the edges anyway before cutting. This will just give you slightly better yields.)

9. KEEP ON ROLLING AND FLATTENING. Once your sheet is looking relatively smooth and strong, start reducing the thickness on the rollers. Do this gradually, step by step, so you don't exert too much stress on the machine. Keep going until you reach your desired thickness.

10. CUT THE DOUGH. Almost there! If your dough still looks a bit rough after sheeting, consider resting it again, though this isn't strictly necessary. Fully rolled-out dough is generally ready to cut right away. Trim the sheet on all sides so it has nice, straight edges, then feed it through whatever cutter you like. For most noodles, the spaghetti cutter (about 2 mm/

½₂ in) is the best choice. You can make the noodles a bit thinner or thicker than this by rolling it out to a thinner or thicker setting before cutting, but if you want really thin noodles (like for the Hard and Thin Noodles on page 77) you need to use a capellini attachment. Feed the dough through carefully, ensuring it doesn't fold in on itself as it goes through the machine, which will result in messed-up noodles.

11. FLOUR AND SHAPE THE DOUGH. High hydration noodles benefit from a moderate dusting of cornflour (cornstarch), which helps keep them from sticking together. If you are making straight noodles, keep them in neat bundles with the strands as aligned as possible. If you are making curly noodles (which is not recommended with low-hydration dough), then you get to temomi them – this is the technique of hand-scrunching, and all you really do is grab the dough in your fists and crumple it up, repeating this process until it forms as much of a curl as you like.

12. REST THE NOODLES. Once the noodles are cut and shaped, they're ready to cook – but resting them again has many benefits. Firstly, noodles straight from the cutter will contain microscopic air bubbles; when these hit boiling water, they puff up like balloons, which makes the noodles thicker and gives them a spongy texture. Secondly, resting will result in more complete hydration, which makes them cook more quickly and evenly, gives them a smoother texture and improves aroma – particularly important if you're making flavoured noodles, such as Toasted Sesame Noodles (page 84).

As they rest, some moisture will evaporate from the noodles, which may condense inside their container and then dampen the noodles, which will mess up their texture and cause them to stick together. To mitigate this, I usually keep the noodles either uncovered or just loosely covered, at room temperature, for a few hours before transferring to the refrigerator.

13. REFRIGERATE THE NOODLES. Kept in a dry, airtight container, fresh noodles will keep in the refrigerator for about a week. You can freeze them, too, but they have a tendency to break once frozen unless handled very gently at all times.

NOODLE TROUBLESHOOTING

When noodles go wrong, it is usually a matter of under- or over-hydration. Under-hydrated noodles won't come together, while over-hydrated noodles can be difficult to cut and are prone to clumping together. If your dough is under-hydrated, probably your best bet is to wrap it well in cling film (plastic wrap) and give it an overnight rest in the refrigerator. This will help it to hydrate and relax. Over-hydrated doughs can be fixed by adding more flour as you sheet it.

Doughs of any kind, noodles included, require less water in warm, humid environments and more when the air is cold and dry. I tested these recipes in my home kitchen, in autumn and winter, when the ambient temperature was about 19–20°C (66–68°F). Not very cold but not warm either, so they should generally work throughout the year. But if you make these noodles in summer – or in a hot professional kitchen – it may be wise to start with a little less water than the recipe calls for. That said, it is much easier to add flour to an over-hydrated dough than to add water to an under-hydrated one. If your dough seems too wet (remember, it should be dry and crumbly), just add more flour, a small spoonful at a time, until it comes to the right consistency.

麺

I originally called this recipe 'all-purpose noodles' but quickly thought better of it. There is no such thing! But when in doubt, go for these ones – they are a good 'Goldilocks' noodle, situated somewhere near halfway between chewy and snappy, and can be either wavy or straight, depending on how they're handled. They are also my preferred choice for cold noodles and even work well in yakisoba.

KEY POINT

The pasta roller marks provided here correlate to decreasing thickness as the value of the number decreases. That is, 1 is the thinnest, and 8 is the thickest. Your pasta roller may be marked in the opposite way, or have no numbers at all, so be mindful of this as you proceed the recipes.

BROTHS
Any, but these work slightly better with lighter broths

RAMEN
Any

Makes 4
Hydration: 37–39%

1 egg
water, as needed (to make 150 g total liquid)
6 g kansui
4 g salt
¼ teaspoon sesame oil
400 g strong white bread flour
8 g vital wheat gluten
cornflour (cornstarch), for dusting

Crack the egg into a bowl and weigh it. In a separate container, pour enough water to make the total mass of the liquid (including the egg) 150 g. Mix the kansui and salt into the water until they dissolve, then use a stick blender to blend in the egg and sesame oil. Follow the instructions for mixing, resting and sheeting on pages 70–72. Roll out to mark 1 or 2 on a pasta roller, then cut using the spaghetti (2 mm/1⁄12 in) attachment. Dust with cornflour and shake off the excess. These can be kept straight or scrunched to form wide or tight curls. Rest and store according to the instructions on page 73.

Springy-Chewy Noodles

These are modelled on the distinctive noodles found in Sapporo-style miso ramen, which have a lovely chew, yellow colour and coily-curly shape that reminds me a bit of telephone headset cables. They are perfect for drawing up the full-bodied, oily soups and varied toppings of Sapporo ramen, but also work well in curry ramen or anything else that has a good amount of sweetness and spice.

BROTHS
Any

RAMEN
Miso
Lazy Goat
  Ragù-Men
Leftover Nando's

Makes 4
Hydration: 38–43%

400 g strong white bread flour	
8 g vital wheat gluten	
8 g whole egg powder	
160 g water	
8 g kansui	
4 g salt	
cornflour (cornstarch), for dusting	

Follow the instructions for mixing, resting and sheeting on pages 70–72. Roll out to mark 2 on a pasta roller, then cut using the spaghetti (2 mm/¹⁄₁₂ in) attachment. Dust with cornflour and shake off the excess. Give them a good firm scrunch to form tight curls. Rest and store according to the instructions on page 73.

NOTE
Noodles in this style (and others) are frequently dyed using riboflavin, aka vitamin B2, which enhances their natural yellowness. Feel free to add this if you like (it is available to buy online). Whatever you do, don't use plant-based food colouring or turmeric to try and achieve the same effect! The alkalinity of kansui makes anthocyanins shift their hues, so the noodles will become a disturbing shade of orangey red, not yellow.

These noodles approximate the kind you get in Kyushu, namely Hakata and Kumamoto ramen. I say 'approximate' because those noodles are made with so little water in the dough (typically 22–25%) they are not possible to replicate with total accuracy at home – but this version comes pretty close. The use of egg white powder helps keep them strong and brittle even at a slightly higher hydration. While these noodles are quite naturally straight, it is important to keep them that way when you store them – they work with thick, Kyushu-style tonkotsu broths by drawing the liquid up through the channels formed between the noodles as they fall parallel to each other from the chopsticks, so even a slight curl will interrupt this effect. Treat them gingerly, carefully folding each portion onto itself, rather than bunching it up into a ball.

BROTHS
Tonkotsu
Pork and Chicken
  Paitan

RAMEN
Garlic Tonkotsu
Half a Pig's Head
Ponzu Reimen
Frozen
  Watermelon and
  Kimchi Reimen

Makes 4
Hydration: 30–32%

400 g strong white bread flour	
10 g egg white powder	
125 g water	
4 g salt	
4 g kansui	
cornflour (cornstarch), for dusting	

Follow the instructions for mixing, resting and sheeting on pages 70–72. Roll out to mark 1 on a pasta roller, then cut using the capellini (1 mm/⅟₃₂ in) attachment. Dust with cornflour and gently shake off the excess. Keep the noodles straight, in neat bundles, rather than in irregular balls. Rest and store according to the instructions on page 73.

つけ麺用の麺
Tsukemen Yō no Men

Thick and Soft Noodles

These noodles are, in a way, the polar opposite of Hakata-style thin and hard noodles, and are intended for use in tsukemen. Their high kansui level means they have a firm bounce once cooked and rinsed with cold water, but the gram flour and moderate hydration give them a suppleness that's easy to chew and eager to absorb broth. Brown rice flour adds a subtle nutty aroma as well as a slippery, slurpable texture. They don't work well sat in most soups for very long, but they are good in *mazesoba* (mixed noodles) or very rich broths, such as tantanmen.

BROTHS
Any, provided it is in tsukemen format

RAMEN
Tsukemen
Lazy Goat Ragù-Men
Yu Xiang Aubergine Mixed Noodles

Makes 4
Hydration: 38–41%

380 g strong white bread flour
10 g brown rice flour
10 g gram flour
150 g water
10 g kansui
4 g salt
cornflour (cornstarch), for dusting

Follow the instructions for mixing, resting and sheeting on pages 70–72. Roll out to mark 4 on a pasta roller, then cut using the spaghetti (2 mm/1⁄12 in) attachment. Dust with cornflour and gently shake off the excess. Keep the noodles straight, in neat bundles, rather than in irregular balls. Rest and store according to the instructions on page 73.

簡単な卵抜きの
万能麺
Kantan na Tamago Nuki no Bannō Men

Easier, Egg-Free
Go-To Noodles

While the Go-To Noodles (page 75) really should be your go-to, because they're so tasty and versatile, they are a little bit annoying to make because of the egg involved. This also makes them no good for vegan ramen. This recipe is a simplified version that addresses both problems. The texture is a little more brittle and the colour is paler, but they're still a decent all-rounder that work well in a variety of bowls.

BROTHS
Any, but these work slightly better with lighter broths

RAMEN
Any

Makes 4
Hydration: 38–40%

400 g strong white bread flour
150 g water
8 g kansui
4 g salt
cornflour (cornstarch), for dusting

Follow the instructions for mixing, resting and sheeting on pages 70–72. Roll out to mark 1 or 2 on a pasta roller, then cut using the spaghetti (2 mm/1⁄12 in) attachment. Dust with cornflour and shake off the excess. These can be kept straight or scrunched to form wide or tight curls. Rest and store according to the instructions on page 73.

麺

Easier, Egg-Free Go-To Noodles

Noodles

Soba-Ramen Hybrid Noodles

麺

蕎麦粉入り麺
Sobako Iri Men

Soba-Ramen Hybrid Noodles

Easily my second-favourite noodle in Japanese gastronomy is soba, the thin, snappy buckwheat noodles which were (I think) Japan's original noodle, owing to the scarcity of wheat for most of Japanese history. I particularly love the nutty aroma of buckwheat, so I wanted to incorporate that into a ramen noodle. After some tinkering I settled on this recipe, with enough buckwheat to add fragrance without interrupting the gluten structure too much. These benefit from several days of resting, which will enhance their aroma as well as texture.

BROTHS
Any, but these are particularly good with chintan or dashi

RAMEN
Old-School Shōyu
Ponzu Reimen
Double Soup

Makes 4
Hydration: 38–40%

| 320 g bread flour |
| 80 g buckwheat flour |
| 16 g vital wheat gluten |
| 2 g salt |
| 6 g kansui |
| 160 g water |
| cornflour (cornstarch), for dusting |

Follow the instructions for mixing, resting and sheeting on pages 70–72. Roll out to mark 2 on a pasta roller, then cut using the spaghetti (2 mm/1⁄12 in) attachment. Dust with cornflour and gently shake off the excess. I prefer these noodles straight, but feel free to temomi them if you like. Rest and store according to the instructions on page 73.

全粒粉二郎系麺
Zenryūfun Jirō-kei Men

Wholegrain Jirō-Style Noodles

One of the key features of Jirō-style ramen is its unusual noodles, which are slightly brown in colour and have an erratic, coarse, ribbony shape. You can replicate this by squashing the noodles haphazardly with a rolling pin. As for the colour of Jirō noodles, that's a result of using a cheap, hard, not very refined flour called Ōshon. I use a small amount of wholemeal (whole-wheat) flour to achieve a similar appearance and pleasantly nutty flavour that works well with the intensity of Jirō ramen.

BROTHS
Any, but these are particularly good with chintan or dashi

RAMEN
Jirō-Style
Tsukemen
Double Soup

Makes 4
Hydration: 40–42%

| 360 g strong white bread flour |
| 40 g strong wholemeal (whole-wheat) flour |
| 160 g water |
| 4 g kansui |
| 4 g salt |
| cornflour (cornstarch), for dusting |

Follow the instructions for mixing, resting and sheeting on pages 70–72. Roll out to mark 3 on a pasta roller, then cut using the spaghetti (2 mm/1⁄12 in) attachment. Dust with cornflour and gently shake off the excess. Temomi each portion of noodles, then lay them on the work surface and flatten them randomly by pressing a rolling pin into their surface. The result should be wavy noodles that are thin in some places and thick in others with an oblong cross-section. Rest and store according to the instructions on page 73.

麺

いりごま麺
Irigoma Men

Toasted Sesame Noodles

Though rare, there are some ramen shops in Japan that offer flavoured noodles, something I first encountered at the Kokura Riverwalk branch of Isshin Furan, now long since closed. They offered an option of noodles with chilli in them, an intriguing way to add spice to the bowl. I later encountered shops that sold noodles made with black pepper and sesame, and the latter really stuck with me as a brilliant idea, as sesame is such a welcome flavour in most ramen, and it echoes both the nuttiness of wheat flour and the richness of animal broths. These noodles are glossy, slick and toothsome, with a irresistible sesame aroma and a colour that reminds me of dark *konnyaku* noodles or good-quality soba.

BROTHS

Any paitan (the oils from the sesame will cloud clear broths)

RAMEN

Miso
Ponzu Reimen
Frozen Watermelon and Kimchi Reimen

Makes 4
Hydration: 38–40%

10 g white sesame seeds	
10 g black sesame seeds	
400 g strong white bread flour	
8 g vital wheat gluten	
162 g water	
6 g kansui	
4 g salt	
cornflour (cornstarch), for dusting	

Stir-fry the sesame seeds in a dry frying pan over a medium heat for about 8–10 minutes until the white ones are rich golden brown and the pan begins to give off a few wisps of smoke. Tip the sesame into a shallow dish and leave to cool completely, then grind to the consistency of fine sand in a spice grinder or mortar. Follow the instructions for mixing, resting and sheeting on pages 70–72, adding the ground sesame to the rest of the dry ingredients at the beginning of mixing. Roll and cut to any thickness you like, then dust with cornflour and shake off the excess. These can be kept straight (better for paitan) or scrunched to form wide or tight curls. Rest and store according to the instructions on page 73.

Egg Noodles

 I wrote in my recipe testing notes for these noodles: 'perfect'. A bold claim, and one that I simply cannot justify. But what I meant was that the noodles do exactly what I wanted them to do, which was to deliver a strong, sulphurous, eggy flavour with a resilient, brittle texture and rich yellow colour. The liquid in these is almost entirely egg, so you'd think they might behave more like a pasta – but our old friend kansui ensures these have a strong structure and bodacious curl. Their up-front egg aroma makes them a good choice for chicken- and soy sauce-forward bowls – and of course, the Full English Tantanmen (page 176).

BROTHS
Any chicken broth

RAMEN
Old-School Shōyu
Old-School Shio
Full English
  Tantanmen

Makes 4
Hydration: 40–43%

2 eggs	
water, as needed (to make 160 g total liquid)	
8 g kansui	
2 g salt	
400 g strong white bread flour	
cornflour (cornstarch), for dusting	

Crack the eggs into a bowl and weigh it. In a separate container, pour enough water to make the total mass of the liquid (including the egg) 150 g. Mix the kansui and salt into the water until they dissolve, then use a stick blender to blend in the egg. Follow the instructions for mixing, resting and sheeting on pages 70–72, minding the special instructions for the egg. Roll out to mark 1 or 2 on a pasta roller, then cut using the spaghetti (2 mm/¹⁄₁₆ in) attachment. Dust with cornflour and shake off the excess. These can be kept straight or scrunched to form curls. Rest and store according to the instructions on page 73.

A BRIEF GUIDE TO SHOP-BOUGHT NOODLES
店で買える麺の案内
MISE DE KAERU MEN NO ANNAI

Even with a mechanised roller, making noodles is not an everyday affair. It's a pretty lengthy process. But you don't have to make your own noodles to make delicious ramen, you just have to source good ones.

No matter what ramen you buy, make sure it contains kansui! Remember, noodles without this are NOT RAMEN and NOT RAMEN is NOT ALLOWED. Look for sodium carbonate, potassium carbonate and/or the E numbers 500 and 501 in the ingredients list. If it doesn't have these, place them back on the shelf and walk away.

The best choice for noodles, if you can get them, are fresh. Some fresh noodles are sold frozen, to be defrosted before cooking, and these are fine too. Beware of ambient fresh noodles sold vac-packed in individual portions. These are intended for dropping directly into soups or stir-fries and they tend to have a soft, crumbly texture.

If you can't get fresh, dried or instant noodles are fine, too. Again, just make sure they contain kansui, and I would also recommend under-cooking them slightly, as they tend to absorb broth more rapidly once boiled. But you should always, always have dried or instant noodles on hand – you never know when the ramen craving will strike.

麺

4

AROMA OILS & FATS

Flavoured oils and fat add extra dimensions of aroma and mouthfeel to ramen, and capture the scents of ingredients differently than if you were to infuse them into water, as in a broth or a tare. Want your pork broth to be more garlicky? Add a garlic oil! Want it more porky? Just add lard! Plus, they're great to have on hand for all sort of other dishes, as well – salads, roast vegetables, stir-fries, etc. They all benefit from a little boost of aroma oil.

香味油

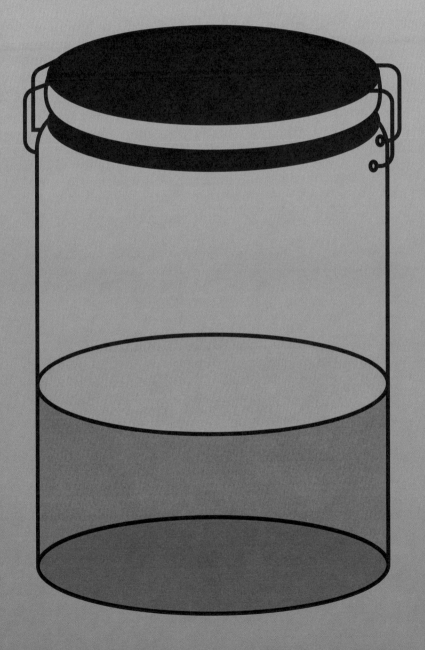

チー油
Chīyu

Schmaltz

Schmaltz is simply rendered chicken fat, known as chīyu in Japan. It makes the surface of any clear broth sparkle like the sea at sunset and imbues the bowl with an irresistible chickeny aroma, even in small amounts. It's a small thing, but it can often make the difference between a *meh* bowl and a *wow* bowl.

BROTHS
Any broths will
  take to this oil,
  but it is
  particularly
  good with
  chickeny
  chintan

RAMEN
Old-School
  Shōyu
Old-School Shio
Curry

You can buy schmaltz, but it's annoyingly rare. Luckily, it is easy to make yourself. All you need is some chicken, some heat and a sieve. Skin is by far the best source of schmaltz I know, but you can use any chicken parts you have. (Butchers will often give you skin for free, so it's well worth asking them.) Simply bake the chicken on a roasting tray in a hot oven (around 160°C fan/350°F), turning frequently, until cooked through and nicely browned, then tip the liquid out through a sieve, decant into a jar or container and keep it in the refrigerator. As it cools, it will separate into a layer of pure, golden fat on top and a layer of gelatinous chicken goo on the bottom. Carefully scoop off the solidified fat, but don't discard the chicken goo – this stuff tastes great, too, and you can add it to any paitan broth for a flavour boost.

If you are rendering fat from skin, the skin will eventually form crackling. I usually drain these off on paper towels and eat them as a snack, but they are a tasty ramen topping. If properly crisped, they remain crunchy even in hot broth.

The schmaltz will keep in the refrigerator for about a month, but I think you'll find yourself getting through it much sooner than that.

Aroma Oils and Fats

ラード
Rādo

Lard

Plentiful and cheap, lard is perhaps more commonly used than schmaltz in ramen. It is much easier to buy than schmaltz, but the refined white blocks sold in supermarkets don't have much aroma. Sometimes this is what you want – a more or less neutral, vaguely piggy fat to add richness or insulation to the bowl. But if you are going for a stronger, porky aroma, it's better to make it yourself.

BROTHS
Any pork-based
 broths

RAMEN
Miso
Jirō-Style
'Nothing
 Special'

The process is the same as making schmaltz. Just get some fatty chunks of pork (the best option is probablyto get pure back fat) and roast them until the fat renders out completely. You can also collect the drippings from roast pork belly or bacon.

However you go about accumulating lard, it can be used in place of vegetable oil in most recipes, to add another dimension of meatiness to your ramen. Because fat can be heated above 100°C (212°F) and retains heat better than water, it can also be warmed in a pan and then poured onto the surface of a bowl of ramen to keep it from cooling down after serving. You will burn your mouth on this, but that's kind of the point. Ramen should be extremely hot – there's nothing more disappointing than tepid ramen. A blanket of scalding hot lard over the top of your broth will absolutely ensure this doesn't happen.

ネギ生姜チー油
Negi Shōga Chīyu

Allium and Ginger Schmaltz

There are several commonalities that link the many styles of ramen; recurring sensory motifs construct and reinforce an unofficial ramen canon and create an impression of what an 'exemplary' ramen might contain, even if no such thing can ever exist. For me, this includes things like the bounce of ramen noodles, the vaguely chemical smell of kansui, the sharpness of spring onions (scallions) and the alluring aroma of fat infused with ginger and garlic. If you were to ask a perfumer to create *eau de ramen*, this is what they might come up with: a versatile oil which enhances virtually any bowl with its combination of rich chicken, musky garlic and warm ginger. It also makes excellent roast potatoes.

BROTHS
Any, but it is perhaps best suited to chicken-based broths

RAMEN
Old-School Shio
Whole Chicken
Clam Miso
 Butter Corn

Makes 100 ml (3.5 fl oz)

100 g (3.5 oz) chicken fat
3 spring onions (scallions), roughly chopped
1 small shallot, finely chopped
4 garlic cloves, crushed
30 g (1 oz) fresh ginger root, very thinly sliced and lightly bashed with a blunt object

Cook everything in a saucepan over a medium-high heat until the vegetables sizzle. Continue to cook until they begin to brown – about 10–12 minutes – then leave to cool to room temperature. Pass through a sieve, pressing down firmly on the veg to extract as much flavour as possible (but be careful not to mash it through the sieve). Keep in the refrigerator for up to a month.

NOTE
This recipe works with any kind of fat. Lard will produce something just as versatile, but in my opinion not as delicious, whereas using vegetable oil, beef dripping or bacon grease is perhaps just as delicious, but not as versatile. Use whatever's handy and see which one you prefer!

柚子胡椒チー油
Yuzu Koshō Chīyu

Yuzu-Koshō Schmaltz

Schmaltz is a wonderful carrier for yuzu-koshō, the pungent paste made from pounding yuzu peel and chillies with salt and leaving them to ferment for a while. This recipe can be made with shop-bought yuzu-koshō (which is always delicious) but I would recommend having a go making it from scratch. Fresh or frozen yuzu peel will give you a more aromatic end product. You can also adjust the heat and flavour to your taste by using different varieties of chilli. I make mine with fruity, fiery Scotch bonnets, a perfect match for the uplifting perfume of yuzu.

BROTHS
Anything chicken- or seafood-based

RAMEN
Old-School Shōyu
Tom Yum Goong
Tokyo Modern

Yuzu-koshō

80–100 g (2.8–3.5 oz) yuzu peel (fresh or frozen), shredded

5–20 g (0.2–0.7 oz) fresh chilles (this will depend on how hot your chillies are and how hot you want the end product to be)

3 g (0.1 oz) salt

Yuzu-koshō schmaltz
Makes 100 g (3.5 oz)

20 g (0.7 oz) yuzu-koshō (homemade or shop-bought)

80 g (2.8 oz) chicken fat

For the yuzu-koshō, pound everything together in a mortar or blitz it in a food processor until a rough paste forms. Press into a small jar or container with the back of a small spoon so that no air pockets remain in the mixture. Press a small piece of cling film (plastic wrap) directly onto the surface of the paste, then cover with a lid. Leave to ferment at room temperature for a week, then transfer to the refrigerator.

Combine both ingredients in a saucepan and heat over a medium heat. When the fat is liquefied, whisk everything together and continue to cook for a few minutes until the yuzu-koshō just begins to sizzle. Remove from the heat, whisk again and leave to cool. Whisk one more time before decanting into a jar or container, then transfer to the refrigerator. This will keep for about a month.

Aroma Oils and Fats

香味油

Aroma Oils and Fats

Garlic Sesame Oil

Like Allium and Ginger Schmaltz (page 92), this is a very 'ramen-esque' oil, making any ramen taste, uh, even more like ramen. What I mean is that sesame and garlic are two aromas I associate very closely with ramen – but be careful with this one, as it can overpower delicate soups. When cooked correctly, this recipe will yield a useful by-product: garlic chips (page 156), which are delicious on all sorts of ramen, particularly Garlic Tonkotsu (page 156).

BROTHS
Any pork broth
Vegetable
 Jirō-Style

RAMEN
Garlic Tonkotsu
Half a Pig's
 Head

Makes 80 ml (2.7 fl oz)

45 ml (3 tablespoons) vegetable oil or lard

60 ml (4 tablespoons) sesame oil

30 g (1 oz) garlic (about 8 cloves), very thinly sliced

Pour the vegetable oil and 1 tablespoon of the sesame oil into a small saucepan and stir in the garlic, ensuring that none of the slices are stuck to each other. Set over a low heat and cook gently for about 15 minutes, stirring often, until the garlic is evenly golden brown (the reason for keeping the heat low is to cook off all of the garlic's moisture before it begins to colour). Once the garlic is lightly browned (we're looking for gold, not bronze), remove it with a slotted spoon, fork or similar, drain on paper towels and leave to cool. Leave the oil to cool for about 10 minutes, then tip into a jar and add the remaining sesame oil. Once the garlic chips have cooled, crush them into small pieces and keep in an airtight container lined with paper towels.

黒マー油

Kuro Māyu

Black Māyu

Māyu is a black oil made from incinerated garlic – it is often confusingly mistranslated as 'black garlic oil', but actual black garlic is an entirely different thing. Māyu is black because the garlic has been burnt to charcoal. I can only assume that it was originally made by accident. Because who in their right mind would burn garlic so catastrophically on purpose? Whenever we made māyu at the restaurant, concerned staff would alert me that something was burning – because it was, very badly!

On its own, māyu tastes just how you might expect it to – like acrid, gritty, burnt garlic. It is, to be honest, kind of nasty on its own. And it doesn't play well with most broths. In fact, I would only recommend it with tonkotsu or vegetable paitan where its sharp bitterness helps balance the richness. It's a bizarre kind of alchemy, and sometimes I feel like tonkotsu is missing something without it. Just remember to switch your extractor on and open the windows when you make this!

BROTHS
Tonkotsu
Pork and Chicken
 Paitan
Vegetable Paitan

RAMEN
Garlic Tonkotsu
Half a Pig's Head

Makes 120 ml (4 fl oz)

80 g (2.8 oz) garlic cloves (peeled weight), thinly sliced
100 ml (3.5 fl oz) vegetable oil
5 tablespoons sesame oil

Place the garlic and vegetable oil together in a saucepan. Heat over a high heat and cook, stirring often, for about 15–20 minutes until the garlic is very, very darkly browned and smoking. At this point, switch off the heat – it will continue to cook and blacken in the oil as it cools. When it's no longer burning hot, tip everything (including the oil) into a blender along with the sesame oil and blend to a smooth purée (unless you have a very powerful blender, like a Vitamix, it won't be totally smooth, but that's okay). Keep in a jar at room temperature and stir well before each use – the garlic charcoal will rapidly settle to the bottom of the jar.

Aroma Oils and Fats

香味油

海苔オイル
Nori Oiru

Nori Oil

A while back I got into an argument with James Chant of Matsudai Ramen (definitely the best ramen shop in Wales, probably the best ramen shop in the whole UK) about nori in ramen. His position: nori is one of the best ramen toppings, because it adds a big whack of oceanic umami and soaks up the broth like a wet tissue. My position: nori is one of the worst ramen toppings, because it ruins the crisp texture of the nori, overpowers the broth with a big whack of oceanic umami and eats like a piece of wet tissue.

HOWEVER. I do love the *aroma* of nori, which is simultaneously fresh and earthy. So I came up with this oil to capture those things, but in a way that interacts much better with the rest of the bowl. It uses aonori rather than nori – a similar, slightly sweeter species of sea vegetable that also has a pleasant green colour and blends better with oil.

BROTHS
Any, but this is particularly good with chicken, seafood and vegetable broths

RAMEN
Old-School Shōyu
Ponzu Reimen
Tokyo Modern

Makes 100 ml (3.5 fl oz)

6 tablespoons vegetable oil
2 tablespoons olive oil
10 g (0.35 oz) aonori flakes

Combine everything in a strong blender and blend until smooth, then decant into a jar. Let the aonori bits settle into the bottom of the jar and leave them there, being careful not to churn them up when spooning the oil onto ramen.

Aroma Oils and Fats

欧風鴨油
Ōfū Kamo Abura

European Duck Fat

This oil uses Western herbs and spices to impart an exotic, pan-European flavour to ramen. It gives pork broths a certain sausagey quality and makes chicken broths taste like a roast chicken dinner. Take your ramen on an occidental adventure!

BROTHS
Any, except seafood-forward broths

RAMEN
Miso
Pizza
Turkey

Makes 80 ml (2.7 fl oz)

100 g (3.5 oz) duck fat
1 star anise
2.5 cm (1 in) piece of leek, roughly chopped
½ teaspoon whole black peppercorns
4 garlic cloves, crushed
15 g (0.5 oz) ginger, thinly sliced
5 thyme sprigs
10 g (0.35 oz) sage

Cook everything except the thyme and sage in a saucepan over a medium-high heat until the vegetables sizzle. Add the thyme and continue to cook for about 5 minutes, then add the sage and cook for another 5–7 minutes until the vegetables begin to lightly brown. Leave to cool to room temperature, then pass through a sieve, pressing down firmly on the veg and spices to extract as much flavour as possible (but be careful not to mash it through the sieve). Keep in the refrigerator for up to a month.

黒胡椒ベーコン油
Kuro Koshō Bēkon Abura

Black Pepper Bacon Grease

In America they sell bacon liberally coated in coarsely ground black pepper. The smell of this sizzling away in the morning is as invigorating as any cup of coffee. The resulting fat is an exquisite ramen topping, bringing a subtle smokiness and the warm, woody quality of pepper. I probably don't have to tell you this is an excellent topping for pork broths, but also for seafood broths and the Full English Tantanmen (page 176).

BROTHS
Any, but it is especially good on seafood-forward broths

RAMEN
Full English Tantanmen
Whole Chicken
Clam Miso Butter Corn

Makes 70–90 g (2.5–3.2 oz)

50 g (1.75 oz) lard
150 g (5.3 oz) smoked streaky bacon, cut into small strips (about 2.5–5 cm (1–2 in) wide)
5 g (0.2 oz) coarsely ground black pepper

Heat the lard and bacon together in a large frying pan over a medium heat. When the bacon is about halfway cooked through – just beginning to brown in places – tip in the black pepper. Continue to cook, stirring frequently, to render as much fat as possible and infuse the pepper. When the bacon is completely browned and crisp, tip everything into a sieve set over a container and press down on the bacon to extract as much peppery grease as possible. Have the bacon as a snack, or use it in the Chicken Caesar Ramen Salad (page 206).

香味油

Aroma Oils and Fats

味付け背脂
Ajitsuke Seabura

Seasoned Back Fat

One of the more unique elements of Jirō-style and its offshoots is a sort of sludge made from semi-rendered, semi-congealed back fat, seasoned with soy sauce or tare. It won't win any beauty contests, but it's really delicious in a decadent, luxurious way, adding a semi-solid, melt-in-your-mouth porkiness to any bowl. Basically, you can feel little flecks of lard on your palate as you slurp, but then they quickly dissolve like delicate pig fat snowflakes. It looks awful; it tastes divine.

BROTHS
Any

RAMEN
Jirō-Style
Miso
Clam Miso
 Butter Corn

Makes ≈175 g (6.2 oz)

250 g (8.8 oz) back fat, cut into roughly 2.5 cm (1 in) square chunks

broth (tonkotsu makes the most sense, but any will do) or water, as needed

2 tablespoons shōyu

½ tablespoon mirin

¼ teaspoon MSG

Add the back fat to a saucepan with enough broth or water to cover by about 2.5 cm (1 in). Bring to the boil and keep at a high simmer for 1 hour, topping up the water as needed, until the fat is very soft. Remove the chunks of fat with a sieve or slotted spoon, then transfer to a bowl or container and mash coarsely with a potato masher or a fork. While still warm, stir in the seasonings and mix well. Keep in the refrigerator for up to 2 weeks.

ベジタリアン
用背脂もどき
Bejitarian Yō Seabura Modoki

Mock Seasoned Back Fat

Vegan Jirō-style is almost an oxymoron, considering how insanely porky the style is. It's pork broth topped with pork topped with pork fat. But really, Jirō-style is an *experience*, as much about the sheer impact of the bowl as it is about any particular ingredients and flavours. It is also, of course, about garlic, which is what this vegan 'back fat' is based on. When garlic is roasted or confited, it goes squishy and absorbs oil well, becoming remarkably similar to the texture of boiled pork fat – and it has a kind of similar funky musk, too. I combine it with silken tofu to reduce its pungency but reinforce its squidgy-creamy texture. Surprisingly, it really works. This is intended for Vegetable Jirō-Style Broth (page 43), of course, but it's great wherever you want to add irregular globs of creamy richness; for example, in a miso ramen.

BROTHS
Tonkotsu
Vegetable
 Jirō-Style

RAMEN
Jirō-Style
Miso
Double Soup

Makes ≈150 ml (5 fl oz)

10 garlic cloves, peeled

3 tablespoons oil

1 tablespoon sesame oil

100 g (3.5 oz) silken tofu

2 tablespoons shōyu

Slowly pan-roast the garlic, whole, in the oils over a low heat until golden brown and soft throughout. Remove with a slotted spoon and leave to cool, then roughly chop or mash them into a mincemeat-like texture. Squish the tofu into a similar size with your hands or a fork, then add this to the oil and slowly fry until most of the moisture evaporates and the tofu barely starts to brown. Cool and combine the tofu and oil with the garlic and shōyu. Keep in the refrigerator for up to a week.

ラー油

Rāyu

Chilli Oil

Chilli oil is one of those things that's like ... why would you bother making it? To answer my own rhetorical question, the reason is because you can fine-tune it exactly to your liking. What follows is a basic recipe for a sort of medium-spicy chilli oil, but with some suggestions to change it up and make it your own.

BROTHS
Any paitan

RAMEN
Any

Makes 300 ml (10 fl oz)

250 ml (8.5 fl oz) vegetable oil

6 garlic cloves, finely chopped

2 small shallots or 1 banana shallot, finely chopped

30 g (1 oz) fresh ginger root, peeled and finely chopped

2 tablespoons hot chilli (hot pepper) flakes

4 teaspoons shichimi

3 tablespoons sesame seeds

50 ml (1.7 fl oz) sesame oil

OPTIONAL ADDITIONS

Add at the beginning of cooking

spring onions (scallions)

citrus peel

black pepper (whole or ground)

fresh chillies

lemongrass

bacon

schmaltz

lard

star anise

Add in the middle of cooking

dried Mexican chillies

curry powder/garam masala

chopped nuts

black sesame seeds

Sichuan pepper/sanshō

miso

Chinese black beans

soy sauce

sugar

yuzu-koshō

smoked paprika

olive oil

Combine the vegetable oil, garlic, shallots and ginger in a saucepan and set over a medium heat. Once the vegetables start to sizzle, let them cook for another 8–10 minutes until they turn golden brown. Remove from the heat, then add the chilli, shichimi and sesame seeds. Leave to cool to room temperature, then add the sesame oil and decant everything into a jar.

NOTE
For a Sichuan-inspired 'hot-and-numbing' flavour, add 10 g (0.35 oz) each of Sichuan pepper and sanshō at the same time you add the chilli flakes. This is particularly delicious on tantanmen.

香味油

5 TOPPINGS

具材

Almost anything can be a ramen topping. But remember, whatever you put on ramen, it must *slurp*, which is to say, it needs to be integrated with the bowl and not just plonked on top of it.

Apart from selecting the right ones and being careful not to overload the bowl, the main thing to consider with toppings is making sure they're all ready to go before the noodles are dropped in. Once the noodles are in the broth, they're on a one-way express train to Soggyville, so the toppings should be administered in a matter of seconds.

基本的な
チャーシューの下味

Kihonteki na Chāshū no Shitaaji

Master Chāshū Marinade

There are so many ways to season chāshū, but for me, it is an opportunity to introduce a bit of sweetness to the bowl. This is my current go-to chāshū tare, which can be used in myriad ways – as a pre-cooking marinade, a braising liquid or a post-cooking marinade – and recipes that use each method follow.

Makes enough for up to 1 kg (2 lb 4 oz) pork or chicken

2 garlic cloves, crushed
15 g (0.5 oz) fresh ginger root, thinly sliced
6 tablespoons shōyu
4 tablespoons sake
4 tablespoons honey (or maltose or golden (light corn) syrup)
4 tablespoons Shaoxing wine
2 tablespoons tamari
2 tablespoons oyster sauce (or mushroom sauce)
1 tablespoon dark brown sugar

Combine all the ingredients in a saucepan and bring to the boil. Boil for a couple of minutes to cook off the alcohol and infuse the garlic and ginger, then remove from the heat and leave to cool.

NOTE
Shaoxing wine brings a distinctive earthy, nutty, somewhat sherry-like flavour. Hon mirin, vermouth, dry sherry or sake that's been open for too long all work well in its place.

煮込み豚肩の
チャーシュー

Nikomi Tonken no Chāshū

Broth-Boiled Pork Shoulder Chāshū

This is perhaps the simplest way to make chāshū: by boiling it in your broth as you make it. The results are soft and supple but also bland, so it's important to give it plenty of time in the marinade after cooking. The meat will also add a little bit of flavour and body to the broth itself, and on that note, you should only cook chāshū using this method in a paitan broth, or at least a broth where clarity is unimportant, because the additional fat will cloud the broth.

Makes 8–12 servings

800 g (1 lb 12 oz) pork shoulder, rind off
1 batch Master Chāshū Marinade

Place the pork in a saucepan and cover with cold water. Set over a high heat and, once it comes to the boil, let it boil for 5 more minutes. Remove the pork and rinse it under tap water to get rid of the scum. Add to the broth of your choice and boil for about 2 hours until fork-tender or 3 hours if you want it even softer – but bear in mind it will be drier and less flavourful at this point. Once the pork is cooked to your liking, place into a container along with the marinade and toss through, then leave to marinate in the refrigerator for at least 2 hours and up to a day, turning the meat occasionally so it is evenly coated.

オーブン焼き豚バラ
チャーシュー

Ōbun Yaki Butabara Chāshū

'Broasted' Pork Belly Chāshū

This technique is how I initially made chāshū. It is what I call 'broasted' – which apparently is actually a method of pressure-frying, but I just use it as a portmanteau of 'braised' and 'roasted'. The meat is about halfway submerged in liquid, with the top exposed to the dry heat of the oven. With belly, this works beautifully, because it keeps the drier, leaner 'bottom' of the belly moist, while the fatty 'top' renders, crisps and caramelises.

Makes 8–12 servings

800 g (1 lb 12 oz) pork belly, rind off
20 g (0.7 oz) kombu
1 can (330 ml/11 fl oz) cola
1 batch Master Chāshū Marinade

Place the pork in a saucepan and cover with cold water. Set it over a high heat and, once it comes to the boil, let it boil for 5 more minutes. Remove the pork and rinse it under tap water to get rid of the scum. Preheat the oven to 160°C fan (350°F). Pierce the meat all over with a thin skewer to allow the braising liquid to penetrate. Place the kombu in the bottom of a roasting dish that fits the pork fairly snugly, then lay the pork on top of it, fat side up. Pour in the cola, then the marinade directly on top of the meat. Cover the dish loosely with foil and braise in the oven for 2 hours, then remove from the heat and continue to cook for another hour, or until you can stick a chopstick into it with very little resistance. Chill in the braising liquid before slicing thinly, against the grain.

Clockwise from upper left, on board: 'Broasted' Belly Chashu, Broth-Boiled Shoulder, Smoked Chashu, Pedro Ximénez Glazed Jowl

具材

Smoked Chāshū

スモーク
チャーシュー
Sumōku Chāshū

The combination of barbecued meat with ramen is irresistible. Some of my favourite ramen is made this way, such as those from Kaubōi Ramen in London or Kemuri Tatsu-ya in Austin. There are other ways to get a smoky flavour into ramen (see Lapsang Souchong-Brined Pork or Chicken Chāshū, page 116), but you can't beat a proper low-and-slow smoke over wood on a barbecue. In addition to infusing the meat with a deep, rich smokiness, the dry heat brûlées the marinade beautifully.

Makes 8–12 servings

800 g (1 lb 12 oz) fatty pork
(belly, neck or jowl work well)

1 batch Master Chāshū Marinade

Place the pork in a saucepan and cover with cold water. Set over a high heat and, once it comes to the boil, let it boil for 5 more minutes. Remove the pork and rinse it under tap water to get rid of the scum. Pierce the meat all over with a thin skewer to allow the marinade to penetrate. Transfer to a container or plastic bag along with the marinade and marinate overnight, tossing the pork once, if necessary, to ensure even marination.

The next day, remove the pork from the liquid and wrap in two layers of kitchen foil. Ignite some charcoal in a kettle or drum barbecue, or similar barbecue capable of indirect heating, then set up the barbecue so the meat is positioned for slow-cooking. (That is, the coals should be placed off to the side or at least 30 cm (12 cm) below the meat.)

Let the barbecue come to 140–150°C (285–302°F). Place the foil-wrapped pork in the barbecue, add some wood chunks, then leave to cook for about 2 hours, turning occasionally and feeding the fire with more charcoal and wood as necessary to maintain a consistent temperature. After 2 hours, carefully remove the pork from the foil wrapping, then place it back on the barbecue and add more wood to the fire. At this point, cook for another hour or so, turning the pork, brushing with the marinade and adding wood frequently, so it is evenly coloured and infused with smoke.

Pedro Ximénez-Glazed Pork Jowl Chāshū

This recipe was inspired by José Pizarro, the great London-based Spanish chef who does very sexy things with pork cheeks and sherry. Sherry isn't common in chāshū recipes, but it is similar in many ways to good-quality mirin, with a brooding fruitiness that works particularly well with pork. As it cooks, it reduces to a kind of rich, raisiny caramel – it is insanely good with the fatty lusciousness and intense flavour of pork jowls. If you have never cooked with this cut before, I encourage you to seek them out – they are called *tontoro* in Japanese, rich with melting, buttery fat. This chāshū is a real luxury, and makes a great little drinking snack on its own.

Makes 6–8 servings

vegetable oil, as needed

2 pork jowls (400–500 g/14 oz–1 lb 2 oz), skinless and trimmed of excess gnarly bits (you'll know what I mean when you see them)

1 onion, quartered

1 garlic clove, crushed

250 ml (8.5 fl oz) Pedro Ximénez sherry

60 ml (4 tablespoons) shōyu

water, as needed (about 100–150 ml/3.5–5 fl oz)

Preheat the oven to 180°C fan (400°F). Pour some oil into a small casserole (Dutch oven) and set on the hob over a high heat. Sear the jowls on both sides until well coloured, along with the onion. Add the garlic, sherry and shōyu to the casserole along with enough water to come up about 1 cm (½ in) shy from the surface of the jowls, then bring to the boil. Place a lid on the casserole and transfer to the oven, then leave to cook for about 2 hours until soft but not collapsing. Place the casserole back on the hob, remove the lid, and bring to a high simmer. Continue to cook for another 30 minutes or so until the liquid has reduced to a thick, jammy glaze, turning the jowls frequently during this time. The meat should be very, very soft – you should be able to cut it with a spoon. Chill the meat in its glaze before slicing and serving.

圧力鍋で作る
パイクー

Atsuryokunabe de Tsukuru Paikū

Pressure Cooker Paikū

One of my favourite ramen shops is Ajisen, in Kumamoto. Ajisen has now become a global chain, but the many franchises both within Japan and abroad pale in comparison to the original shop, which produces ramen of an entirely different calibre. True to the Kumamoto style, their tonkotsu-based soups are rich with roasted garlic, and a particularly unique offering there is something called *paikū*. This, I believe, is a corruption of the Chinese word for spareribs and refers to the cartilage that runs perpendicular to the ribs themselves. After a long braise – or, in my version, a rapid pressure-cook – this cartilage becomes wibbly and jellified, almost like a solid iteration of the broth. It's a delightful texture and flavour, soft squishiness barely held together in a mesh of lean rib meat.

Makes about 6 servings

rib tip cartilage from 2 racks of ribs
vegetable oil, as needed for searing
2 garlic cloves, crushed
2 spring onions (scallions), cut in half
15 g (0.5 oz) garlic, thinly sliced
1 star anise
4 tablespoons shōyu
2 tablespoons sugar
1 tablespoon Worcestershire sauce
½ teaspoon salt
½ teaspoon MSG
water, as needed (400–500 ml/ 14–17 fl oz)

Using a sharp, heavy knife, cut the cartilage into chunks about 5 cm (2 in) wide – you'll get about 6 chunks out of each strip of cartilage. Heat the oil in the bottom of a pressure cooker over a medium-high heat, then sear the cartilage on both sides, working in batches so you don't crowd the pan. Once all the cartilage has been seared, add it back to the pot along with all of the other ingredients, including enough water to barely cover the meat. Cook on full pressure for 1 hour, then remove from the heat and let the pressure dissipate naturally (don't open the valve). Keep in the cooking liquid until ready to use; to reheat from chilled, bring back to the boil in their liquid.

NOTE

The rib cartilage often has a flap of lean meat attached to it – I could be mistaken, but I believe this is the pig's equivalent to a flank steak, and it does not like to be pressure-cooked, becoming tough and stringy. If it's there, trim this flap off, ensuring that you only use the cartilage and the meat that directly surrounds it.

煙茶漬け
チャーシュー

Encha-zuke Chāshū

Lapsang Souchong-Brined Pork or Chicken Chāshū

Lapsang souchong tea is a brilliant ingredient to have on hand to add a smoky flavour to foods without busting out the smoker. When used in a brine, the tannins in the tea also have the unique effect of tenderising the meat. This works well for pork or chicken, but the cooking methods are very different – see below.

Makes 8–12 servings

4 lapsang souchong teabags
400 ml (14 fl oz) just-boiled water
20 g (0.7 oz) salt
2 tablespoons sugar
100 ml (3.5 fl oz) shōyu
3 tablespoons mirin
800 g (1 lb 12 oz) pork belly or about 4 chicken breasts

Place the teabags in a container large enough for the meat and pour over the boiled water. Stir in the salt and sugar, then leave to steep and cool down for about 30 minutes. Add the shōyu and mirin, then place the meat in the brine. Leave to soak overnight, turning the meat once to ensure even brining.

FOR PORK

Preheat the oven to 160°C fan (350°F). Remove the pork from the marinade and pat it dry. Cook in a roasting tray covered with foil for 2 hours. Remove the foil and cook for another hour until fork-tender. Chill thoroughly before slicing and serving.

FOR CHICKEN

Preheat the oven to 180°C fan (400°F). Remove the chicken from the marinade and pat it dry. Place in a roasting tray, uncovered, and cook for 20–30 minutes, or until the internal temperature reaches 65°C (149°F) on a probe thermometer. Alternatively, gently pan-fry the chicken in a little oil or chicken fat over a very low heat until done. Chill thoroughly before slicing and serving.

(ピリ辛)肉味噌

(Pirikara) Nikumiso

(Spicy) Nikumiso

This is a versatile yet simple topping that acts as both an additional seasoning and a protein. It's basically pork mince (or any mince (ground meat), really) bound together with miso and a variety of other sweet and umami seasonings, and I usually like to make it spicy, too – but this is optional. It works on pretty much any kind of ramen but I think it's best in bowls that are on the richer side.

Makes enough for up to 8 bowls

50 g (1.75 oz) lard
(or other animal fat)

1 onion, finely chopped

60 g (2 oz) red miso – red or barley miso is preferable

2 tablespoons tomato purée (paste)

4 garlic cloves, finely chopped

1 fresh red chilli (optional – choose the variety based on how much spice you want), finely chopped

2 teaspoons chilli (hot pepper) flakes (optional)

2 cm (¾ in) piece of fresh ginger root, peeled and finely chopped

1 tablespoon toasted sesame seeds

¼ teaspoon white pepper

250 g (8.8 oz) minced (ground) pork

1 tablespoon sugar

1 teaspoon sesame oil

Melt the lard in a frying pan set over a medium-high heat and add the onion. Sauté until lightly browned, then add the miso, tomato purée, garlic and chilli (if using). Stir into the fat and leave to cook for 2–3 minutes without stirring so the miso and tomato begin to caramelise. Add the chilli flakes (if using), ginger, sesame and pepper. Sauté for another 2–3 minutes, then add the pork mince and sugar. Continue to stir-fry for another 8 minutes or so until the pork is cooked through and lightly browned. Remove from the heat and add the sesame oil. Keep in the refrigerator for up to a week.

Clockwise, from top: Confit Turkey Leg, Tare-Poached Chicken Thigh, Lapsang Souchong-Brined Chicken and Shiokōji Chicken

Toppings

Shiokōji Chicken

塩麹漬け鶏チャーシュー
Shiokōji-zuke Tori Chāshū

Shiokōji is a paste made from salt and rice inoculated with kōji, the essential Japanese fungus used in the fermentation of sake, soy sauce, miso and numerous other Japanese foods and seasonings. It tastes like a more stark version of miso, a pure, sweet, slightly boozy flavour of actively fermenting rice and salt. It works well as a marinade not just because of its flavour but also because its enzymatic activity helps tenderise meats and lightly pickle vegetables. It makes for wonderfully succulent, sweet chicken chāshū, especially if you cook it under a hot grill (broiler) to caramelise its sugars.

Makes 8 servings

30 g (1 oz) shiokōji
30 g (1 oz) white miso
2 tablespoons mirin
4 chicken thighs, boneless and skin on

Stir together the seasonings until a smooth paste is formed. Toss the thighs through this mixture and leave to marinate for at least an hour or overnight. Heat the grill (broiler) to high and position an oven rack about 13–15 cm (5–6 in) from the grill. Line a baking sheet with foil and place the chicken on it, skin side down. Grill (broil) for about 10 minutes, then turn the chicken over and grill for a further 20 minutes, or until the skin is lightly blackened and the thighs are cooked through. Rest for several minutes before slicing and serving.

煮込み鶏もも肉
チャーシュー
Nikomi Tori Momoniku Chāshū

Tare-Poached Chicken Thigh Chāshū

One of the nice things about using chicken rather than pork for chāshū is that it cooks far more quickly, and one of the simplest ways to make chāshū is to simply poach chicken in tare. The only problem with this method is that it throws the tare itself out of whack, depleting its salinity so it has to be re-seasoned with more soy sauce. At the restaurant we did this to taste, which was admittedly inconsistent, but I actually came to embrace that inconsistency. Everybody's palate is different, and who was I to be the arbiter of seasoning anyway? As long as the dish isn't patently too salty – which is difficult to rectify – it's fine! The diner (or the chef) can always add more soy sauce or salt if they want to.

Makes 8 servings

4 chicken thighs, boneless but skin on

400–500 ml (14–17 fl oz) shōyu tare of your choice

Combine the chicken and tare in a saucepan; don't worry if the chicken is not totally submerged. Place a lid on the pan and bring to the boil over a high heat.

Once the tare is boiling, reduce the heat to medium-low and simmer for 15–18 minutes, turning the chicken over once halfway through cooking. Remove the chicken from the tare with a slotted spoon and leave to cool thoroughly before slicing and serving. Pass the tare through a sieve when decanting into a container.

Confit Turkey Leg

Turkey is almost never used in ramen in Japan, presumably because turkey is not widely eaten. It is readily available outside of Japan, though, and it makes a killer ramen topping. You can use the breast (page 185) but I have always been a dark meat man, and my favourite way to prepare it for ramen is by confiting it in a flavourful fat – which can then be used as an aroma oil. Bonus!

Makes about 10 servings

1 turkey leg (about 800 g/1 lb 12 oz), thigh and drumstick separated
1 tablespoon salt
1 tablespoon light brown sugar
1 teaspoon garlic granules
1 teaspoon smoked paprika
¼ teaspoon pepper
150 ml (5 fl oz) sesame oil
150 g (5.3 oz) animal fat of your choice
150 g (5.3 oz) unsalted butter
2 star anise
1 garlic bulb, halved
1 rosemary sprig (optional)
1 handful of sage leaves (optional)

Rub the turkey all over with the salt, sugar, garlic granules, paprika and pepper. Leave to cure overnight in the refrigerator, then rinse the rub off the turkey under cold running water, drain well and pat dry with a clean cloth or paper towels. Preheat the oven to 140°C fan (325°F). In an ovenproof casserole (Dutch oven) or dish that will just fit the turkey leg, combine all of the remaining ingredients and set over a medium heat. When the solid fats have melted and the garlic and herbs are just beginning to sizzle, carefully lower in the turkey meat. Place a lid on the dish and transfer to the oven. Cook for 3 hours, turning the meat over once halfway through. Leave the meat to cool in its fat before portioning and serving. The fat can be used as an aroma oil and will keep for several weeks in the refrigerator. If it is kept submerged in the fat, the turkey should also keep for at least 2 weeks, but if any of the meat is exposed to air it will spoil.

代替肉の
チャーシュー

Daitainiku no Chāshū

Mock Meat Chāshū

I've experimented with various plant-based protein toppings to replace chāshū in vegan bowls, but ultimately I've found the best solution to this problem is perhaps the most obvious: traditional Chinese mock meat. This comes in many forms, but the ones that work best are those that come as larger chunks or whole 'cuts', as opposed to mince or small pieces. Try to avoid varieties that are heavily spiced or flavoured. The use of five-spice powder in mock duck in particular can be very overpowering and out of place in a bowl of ramen.

mock meat
Master Chashu Marinade

To make mock meat into chāshū, simply follow the cooking instructions on the package, or the 'broth boiling' method on page 110, before resting in the marinade. It may go without saying, but if you are trying to keep everything vegan, you need to use mushroom sauce instead of oyster sauce and some sort of syrup instead of honey. Various types of mock meat absorb marinades at different rates, so taste it every 2 hours or so to see how it's coming along.

具材

Wontons

This is a straightforward, basic wonton recipe using shop-bought wrappers and mild seasonings that will match well with almost any ramen you drop it into. Why shop-bought wrappers? Because wontons for ramen should be ethereally thin – it's *very* hard to roll them thin enough at home. However, I would advise buying specifically Japanese wonton wrappers, as Chinese wonton pastry tends to contain egg and high levels of kansui, which make them yellow and quite firm. Wontons for ramen should be white in colour and very delicate and silky. They are a carrier not only for the filling but also for the broth, which should rapidly soak into the dough.

Any mince (ground meat) you like can be used for this recipe; pork or chicken are the traditional choices, but I do love a good prawn (shrimp) wonton. The seasonings are kept deliberately mild for maximum compatibility with various kinds of ramen – feel free to increase them or change them up as you like.

**Makes 30 wontons
(enough for 6–10 bowls of ramen)**

200 g (7 oz) mince (ground meat) of your choice – chicken, pork, prawn (shrimp) all work

1 garlic clove, finely grated

2.5 cm (1 in) piece of leek (from the white end), very finely chopped

5 g (0.2 oz) fresh ginger root, peeled and very finely chopped

⅛ teaspoon salt

1 big pinch of MSG

1 pinch of white pepper

2 tablespoons panko

a few drops (literally drops) sesame oil

30 shop-bought Japanese wonton or gyoza wrappers

Combine all of the ingredients except the wrappers and mix well. Place a small spoonful of the mince mixture in the centre of each wrapper and dampen the outside of each wrapper with a little bit of water. Fold two of the opposing corners of each wrapper onto each other, then tuck in the remaining corners and make three little pleats to seal. Set aside on a tray until ready to use. If not using immediately, cover and refrigerate for up to one day, or freeze for up to 6 months. To cook, simply boil in water for 2–3 minutes, remove with a slotted spoon, drain well and drop into your ramen.

具材

AJITAMA AND THE EGG MATRIX
味付け卵の案内
AJITSUKE TAMAGO NO ANNAI

Ah, the ramen egg: perhaps the single topping most fetishised by casual slurpers. While ramen geeks and professionals are usually more focused on the finer points of broths, tare and noodles, it's those eggs that seem to be the thing most customers are enamoured with. And who can blame them? A perfect ramen egg (*ajitsuke tamago*, or *ajitama* for short) is truly rapturous – the salty sweetness of the marinade, the firm and bouncy white, the rich and jammy yolk – it is how we always *want* eggs to taste. And luckily (and unlike many other elements of ramen) they are relatively easy to make – but there are some guidelines.

Everybody has a slightly different idea of how they want their ramen eggs to turn out. Some people like them very runny. In old-school ramen shops in Japan, where eggs are sort of a bonus and sometimes an afterthought, they're often hard-boiled. Some are super dark and salty, others are more lightly marinated. For me, the perfect ramen egg has a mostly set yolk with very little left that's still totally liquid – runny yolk simply dissolves into the broth and gets lost. I want to be able to really sink my teeth into that yolk and experience it on its own. But it's up to you, and the visual 'egg matrix' that follows will help guide you towards egg perfection.

But the boil is only part of the battle. There are things to consider before you even switch on the kettle.

Bear in mind that salty marinades will further cure and set the egg – so a finished ajitama will be slightly less runny than ones that are freshly boiled and peeled.

1
EGG SELECTION

EGG FLAVOUR

I tested a lot of different varieties of eggs in the run-up to opening my restaurant, and I found no consistent difference in the flavour between 'cheap' free-range eggs and more expensive boutique or heritage breed eggs. However, pricier eggs almost always have a better yolk colour, which brings us to...

YOLK COLOUR

For me, and for many diners, a darker, bolder-coloured yolk is simply more aesthetically pleasing, and I think it conveys a sense of higher quality. But it is, ultimately, pure aesthetics.

EGG PEELABILITY

Eggs destined for ramen should be easy to peel. If they aren't, you'll end up with ugly, dented eggs, or a lot of unusable breakages. Ease of peeling also seems to be unrelated to egg price or quality, but there are two factors I've found that do seem to impact peelability: egg age and doneness. In general, in my experience (and I do have a lot of experience – I personally used to peel at least 30 dozen eggs per week at the restaurant), softer-boiled eggs are more difficult to peel than harder ones, which makes sense: the more cooked the white, the firmer it is, and therefore less prone to breaking.

As for age: **older eggs are easier to peel**. Eggshells are slightly porous, and over time the water content of the white inside slowly evaporates away, which makes the white shrink and pull away from the inner walls of the shell. The tiny air gap that forms between the white and the shell makes them easier to peel. So how do you know how old your eggs are? The easiest way is to check the best-by date. Anything within a week of this date should be noticeably more peelable. However, in old eggs the yolk will slowly sink to the bottom of the egg, so make sure they are kept pointed-side down to keep the yolk centred.

2
BOILING

Once you've selected your eggs you can prepare them for boiling. Firstly, **have your marinade ready and at room temperature or colder** – if you put your eggs into a hot marinade they will continue to cook. Next – and this is optional, but helpful – **pierce the shells on their wider, rounder end with an egg piercer**, which are available online. This will make them less prone to bursting during the boil and help produce a rounder egg that's also easier to peel.

Now, prepare your boiling set-up. **Use a large pan of water for this, set over your strongest burner** – I would say a water level of at least four times the volume of the number of eggs you're cooking. If you use too little water, or too weak a flame, adding cold eggs or even room temperature eggs will interrupt the boil, ruin the cooking time and result in inconsistent eggs. You may want to **add a big glug of vinegar** to the water, which both weakens the shell and firms the white, making them easier to peel – although this is not necessary if you are confident you have chosen eggs with high peelability.

Have a large container (the larger the better) filled with cold water at the ready, which you will use to immediately drop the temperature of the eggs after boiling and halt the cooking. If you are doing a lot of eggs consider adding ice, though if this is not practical you can simply add more cold running water to the container once your eggs are in it, so it doesn't warm up.

Use a metal strainer or colander to hold the eggs so you can lower them into and take them out of the water all at once. (At the restaurant we used deep-fryer baskets, which held 30 eggs and fit into our noodle boiler perfectly.) **Have the water at a consistent, rolling boil** on your strongest burner and set a timer for however long you like, typically between 6½–8½ minutes. Check the photo on the following page for a visual guide – a lot of egg recipes call for boiling for a specific amount of time, usually 6½–7 minutes, but as you can see, 6½ minutes is disastrous for very large or even large eggs, especially if kept in the refrigerator. Unless you want your eggs *super* runny and don't mind a bit of un-set white. They're your eggs, so it's up to you!

Lower in the eggs and hit start on the timer. Remove the eggs when the timer is up and tip them into the cold-water bath. After the eggs have been in the water for 1–2 minutes, give them a stir to redistribute the water temperature.

3
PEELING

Once the eggs are chilled, peel them. **Crack them by giving them several firm whacks all around the egg on your work surface, particularly on either 'tip' of the egg** – this might be complete nonsense, but I think the impact of a solid blow rather than a delicate tap helps to force the shell away from the white due to a sudden blast of pressure. Again, I have no idea if that's true, but this is how I managed to peel 360 eggs in 58 minutes and 25 seconds (yes, I timed it) with only 14 breakages. Your results may vary, but eggs are more robust than you might think. Whatever you do, **never break your eggshells by tapping them on a corner of a container or work surface** – the edge can cut the egg rather than crack it, which can damage the white and make it harder to peel.

It is easiest to peel eggs underwater, probably because the water also helps to gently push the shell away from the white. By the way, if an egg is not cooperating – the shell or inner membrane stubbornly clinging to the white, the white itself breaking or flaking away – let it go. **Some eggs just don't want to be peeled, so to hell with them.** Have them on toast. One every now and again is not a big deal, but if it is a consistent problem, consider changing your brand of eggs, your cook time or the amount of vinegar in your water – or all of the above.

It should be noted that what you're doing when you peel eggs isn't separating the shell from the white, but actually separating the membrane (or 'cuticle') from the white. This may seem like a pointless thing to distinguish, but it will help you peel your eggs. **The shell will never release cleanly unless you tear the membrane and loosen it from the white** and, once you do that, peeling the entire egg becomes much easier. Also remember to **remove all the stubborn bits of cuticle** that might be clinging to the white – the marinade will not penetrate those bits as well and they will appear discoloured in the final egg.

4
MARINATION

Once your eggs are peeled, you did it! All that's left to do is marinate them. Specific recipes follow, but marination will generally take about 6–36 hours. Less than this and they will likely be under-seasoned and not very firm. More than this and they tend to be too salty and a bit rubbery. For me the 'sweet spot' is always about 24 hours, but it depends on the marinade, the cook on the egg and your personal preference. Be warned that seriously over-marinated eggs (for around 48 hours or more) may also begin to turn soft and crumbly.

To ensure even coverage of the marinade, **drape a folded-up piece of paper towel over the surface of the eggs** once they're settled in the container. Alternatively, **you can marinate your eggs in a plastic bag,** which will help the eggs' surfaces maintain contact with the liquid all over. **Gently stir or toss the eggs through their marinade periodically to avoid 'bald spots' from where your eggs were touching each other.** Unless you're planning to eat them within a few hours, keep the eggs in the refrigerator until ready to use.

To serve the eggs, have them at room temperature or slightly warm – at the restaurant we would do this by retrieving a dozen or so eggs at a time and pouring boiling water over them, which is enough to heat them up without risking over-cooking. You can also heat them up gently in a saucepan in their own marinade, but be cautious with this method. Most ajitama in Japan are served unsliced, but **if you do want to slice them, a length of thin fishing wire tied to a fixed part of your kitchen (or something very heavy) is the tool of choice.** (A knife, no matter how sharp and thin, will make a mess of the yolk.)

I have just written about 1,700 words on boiling eggs, but incredibly, there is still more to say. For this, I would direct you to Preston Landers' comprehensive article on the subject, which I myself have learned quite a bit from. Just google **'Preston Landers egg'** – have a read, then go and cook some eggs!

All egg marinade recipes yield enough for at least 6 medium or large eggs.

FRIDGE TEMPERATURE　　**ROOM TEMPERATURE**　　**FRIDGE TEMPERATURE**

MEDIUM EGGS

LARGE EGGS

EXTRA LARGE EGGS

具材

基本的な醤油卵
の下味

Basic Soy Sauce Egg Marinade

Kihonteki na Shōyu Tamago no Shitaaji

This is a typical, simple egg marinade recipe that's easy to remember and also very easy to customise, as well, with different ratios, different types of soy sauce, dashi instead of water, or added flavourings such as ginger, garlic and spring onion (scallion). Feel free to experiment.

Makes enough for 6 eggs

5 g (0.2 oz) kombu, cut into small pieces, or ¼ teaspoon MSG

4 tablespoons shōyu

3 tablespoons water

2 tablespoons mirin

1 tablespoon sugar

Stir everything together. If you're using kombu, let it sit for 1 hour to infuse before using. Use as a marinade for eggs according to the guide on page 129.

紅茶卵の下味

Tea Egg Marinade

Kōcha Tamago no Shitaaji

This is my oldest and oddest egg marinade recipe, but still one of my favourites. The use of lapsang souchong (also tasty in chāshū, page 116) gives the eggs a smoky, almost meaty flavour, but different teas work as well. Be aware that if you steep the tea too hot, or leave the eggs in the marinade for too long, the tannins will cause the egg whites to break down and become mushy. I recommend cold-infusing the tea and marinating for no more than 24 hours.

Makes enough for 6 eggs

1 star anise

150 ml (5 fl oz) just-boiled water

4 tablespoons shōyu

2 tablespoons mirin

2 tablespoons rice vinegar

1 lapsang souchong teabag

Place the star anise into a heatproof jar or container and pour in the boiled water. Add the remaining seasonings and stir, then add the teabag. Leave to infuse for about an hour, then use to marinate boiled eggs according to the guide on page 129.

ニンニク味噌卵
の下味

Ninniku Miso Tamago no Shitaaji

Garlic Miso Egg Marinade

Miso-marinated ajitama are rare in Japan, but I am not sure why. They're an interesting alternative to the usual soy sauce- or salt-based marinades, and the range of flavours found in miso means they're easily customisable. This recipe rounds out the miso with water, mirin and a nice whack of garlic. As you can imagine, they're perfect for miso ramen.

Makes enough for 6 eggs

½ garlic clove, grated
6 tablespoons water
4 tablespoons miso (any kind, but I tend to prefer darker varieties)
2 tablespoons mirin
1 teaspoon sesame oil

Whisk together all the ingredients until no lumps of miso remain. Use to marinate boiled eggs according to the guide on page 129.

温泉卵
Onsen Tamago

Onsen Eggs

Onsen – or hot spring – eggs, are the delightfully jellied eggs created by cooking eggs in their shells at a low temperature, around 63–65°C (145–149°F). By far the easiest and most reliable way to make these is with an immersion circulator and, if you have one, all you need to do is fill it up, switch it on, let it come to temperature, add your eggs and wait. I've always done them for 1 hour at 64°C (147°F). There are countless different combinations that work, apparently, and give slightly different results in terms of the consistencies of the yolk and white. I've seen anywhere from 63°C (145°F) for 1 hour 30 minutes to 75°C (167°F) for 13 minutes. Play around if you like –1 hour at 64°C (147°F) works for me.

If you don't have an immersion circulator, you need to find another way to hold that temperature. I have never tried to do this, because I have a water bath and also, you know, life's too short. But the most convincing and least tedious method I've seen comes from the always-reliable website *Just One Cookbook*. Google it.

The finished eggs will likely contain a loose, watery layer surrounding the set, jellified white. Crack the eggs into a bowl and then use a slotted spoon to remove the eggs, so the white liquid doesn't go into your ramen (it tastes fine – it just looks bad).

Onsen eggs are an essential topping for *aburasoba* (oil noodles, page 209) and are also very pleasant in light, dashi-forward soups.

具材

Other Protein-Based Toppings

Apart from the previous pages, there are many other protein-y items that taste good on ramen. Here are some of my favourites:

'Nduja
ンドゥイヤ Nduiya

Some ramen is garnished by a dollop of spicy miso paste, popularised by the Yamagata shop Ryū Shanghai. 'Nduja, the Calabrian pâté of pork, tripe and no small amount of fiery pickled red chillies, makes an exceptional topping in a similar vein, melting into the broth as you slurp and making it porkier, saltier and spicier all at once.

Narutomaki & Kamaboko
ナルト巻き・蒲鉾

Narutomaki are the iconic fish cakes with a frilly edge and a pink spiral in the middle. They are a cute protein bonus rather than a substantial topping. The similar kamaboko are seldom used in ramen – they're more of an udon thing – but they are a key part of the stir-fry that adorns chanpon.

Tofu
豆腐

Silken tofu makes for a reasonably good vegan approximation of chāshū, with a similar luscious, fall apart-y texture. It is best if you drain it well, slice it, fry it and marinate it first – just like you might with chāshū.

Shellfish
貝類物 Kairuimono

Occasionally, bivalves turn up in ramen, which do double duty in terms of flavour: they add their juice to the broth (page 38), and their meat as a topping. Clams are the classic choice, but mussels and oysters are also delicious.

Cheese
チーズ Chīzu

All sorts of grated cheeses work well on ramen. Mozzarella is a good, neutral choice that helps bind toppings to the noodles, but more flavourful options are tasty, too. Parmesan is probably my favourite; it has a particular affinity with miso and is good on spicy, garlicky ramen.

麻辣スパイス
Mārā Supaisu

Mala Mix

This is a dry seasoning which can be deployed onto any unsuspecting bowl to turn it into an electrical fire of hot-and-numbing flavour. But it isn't just a sensory assault; it also has a delightful, complex, uplifting fruity-herbal aroma. It is perhaps most at home on tantanmen (page 175) but is also delicious on rich miso- and paitan-based soups. But be careful with this – a little bit goes a long way!

Makes 70 g (6.2 oz)

1 tablespoon Sichuan pepper
2 tablespoons white sesame seeds
2 tablespoons black sesame seeds
1 teaspoon cumin seeds
1 teaspoon caraway seeds
2 tablespoons chilli (hot pepper) flakes
1½ teaspoons ground sanshō
2 teaspoons shichimi
2 teaspoons gochugaru
2 teaspoons aonori flakes (optional)
1 teaspoon sugar
½ teaspoon ground white pepper
¼ teaspoon MSG
1 pinch of salt

Place the Sichuan pepper, sesame seeds, cumin and caraway in a dry frying pan and set over a medium heat. Toast the spices for about 8 minutes, stirring frequently, until the sesame seeds are golden brown (if you are using toasted sesame seeds, they should be more of a bronze). Tip everything out of the pan and leave to cool to room temperature, then transfer to a spice grinder or mortar and crush to a coarse, sandy consistency. Combine this mixture with all of the remaining ingredients, stirring well. Keep in a jar at room temperature for up to 3 months (it won't go off, but it will start to lose aroma).

NOTE

The quality of Sichuan pepper varies widely, and this will make a difference in the finished product. In particular, try to get Sichuan pepper which has a vibrant red colour and, ideally, has already had the hard black seeds removed – the seeds are flavourless, and have a gritty, unpleasant texture. If you have Sichuan pepper with the seeds in, you'll have to painstakingly remove them from each husk individually.

合わせ魚粉
Awase Gyofun

Seafood Sawdust

In Japan, dried fish powders called *gyofun* are used in some ramen to add a blast of seafood aroma and deep umami, as well as an interesting graininess to the broth. These are hard to get here in the UK, with the exception of katsuo powder, which is made as a by-product of shaving katsuobushi. I was invited by one of the UK's biggest Japanese food wholesalers to see their katsuobushi-shaving operation in Enfield, and the process was very cool. They run the dried logs of katsuobushi through these terrifying industrial shaving machines, basically like a sawmill, producing fine flakes as well as a coarse katsuo dust. Hence the name of this garnish: seafood sawdust.

While working in Brixton, I combined this with West African dried and smoked prawns (shrimp) to make the evolved form of seafood sawdust. It is one of my favourite ramen toppings ever; a small spoonful adds a huge blast of aroma and umami.

Makes 50 g (1.75 oz)

20 g (0.7 oz) West African dried smoked prawns (shrimp) (or ordinary dried prawns or niboshi)

40 g (1.4 oz) katsuobushi

Preheat the oven to 180°C fan (400°F) and lay the prawns out on a baking tray. Roast the prawns for 8–10 minutes until aromatic and visibly darker in colour. Remove from the oven and leave to cool completely. Transfer to a blender and blend very well until a fine powder is formed, then add the katsuobushi and continue to blend until that is pulverised, too. Pass the powder through a sieve to catch any big, hard bits and transfer to a jar. Provided the jar is well sealed, this will keep for about a month at room temperature, after which it will begin to smell like ammonia.

拉麺胡椒
Rāmen Koshō

Ramen Pepper

I first encountered the GS Foods product 'ramen pepper' in Hakodate, where it sits on the counters of many of the city's ubiquitous shio ramen shops. It is a very simple spice blend designed to underscore the allium notes of old-school Chinese-style soups. But it's also great on fried chicken or popcorn!

Makes 20 g (0.7 oz)

4 teaspoons ground black pepper

2 teaspoons ground white pepper

2 teaspoons onion granules

1½ teaspoons garlic granules

Combine all the ingredients and mix well. Keep in a jar for up to 2 months.

具材

SLURP YOUR VEGETABLES: A FIELD GUIDE TO PLANT-BASED RAMEN TOPPINGS
野菜トッピングの案内
YASAI TOPPINGU NO ANNAI

While eating ramen probably isn't a great strategy for getting your five-a-day, vegetables and fungi play an important part in bringing contrast and colour to the bowl. Here are some key veg toppings, with a note on each one.

1. SPRING ONIONS (RINGS OR SHREDS)
Perhaps the most ubiquitous topping there is. Use a very sharp knife when cutting so that you don't damage them. Keep shredded spring onions (scallions) in iced water (or just in water in the refrigerator) to make them curl up.

2. LEEKS (DICE OR SHREDS)
Spring onions' (scallions') tougher big bro. Use only the tender inner layers and never the green parts. Diced leeks benefit from a brief simmer in hot broth to soften them.

3. CHIVES
Spring onions' sweeter lil' bro. Can be finely chopped, or kept chunkier for added texture and a more potent oniony flavour.

4. NIRA
Also called Chinese chives or garlic chives. They appear in spicy or old-school Chinese-style soups. Their garlicky musk becomes stronger the longer they sit after being sliced.

5. SHIITAKE
Rehydrated shiitake mushrooms from making dashi (page 38) can be de-stemmed, sliced and served on ramen as is, marinated, or as part of a stir-fry. They are excellent broth absorbers.

6. KIKURAGE
Crunchy wood ear mushrooms, sold shredded and dried. Interestingly, their Japanese name means 'tree jellyfish'. Rehydrate them by simmering in a mixture of about 70% water and 30% soy sauce.

7. ENOKI AND SHIMEJI
Common Japanese mushrooms with a mellow flavour. Enoki are particularly interesting in ramen because of how their texture mimics noodles. Shimeji are best as part of a stir-fry.

8. BRAISED MUSHROOMS
Meaty, fibrous mushrooms such as oyster mushrooms can be cooked down à la chāshū in a sweet and salty marinade, making for a substantial topping in vegan bowls.

9. CHILLI THREADS
Called *ito tōgarashi* in Japanese, these are mild dried red chillies that have been fed through a special machine to make fine threads. Gently toasting them in a dry frying pan will improve both their aroma and texture.

10. NORI
A classic garnish which lends a strong seaweedy aroma to the bowl, while acting as a supple sponge for broth. More on page 100.

11. WAKAME
Leafy sea greens are most commonly found in miso soup. Their strong flavour works well in shōyu-based bowls, but they are also found in curry ramen (page 164) and ramen that showcases seafood.

12. SESAME SEEDS
Must be toasted. Typically white is used, but black are okay, too.

13. BEAN SPROUTS
Fantastic for adding textural contrast to bowls. Simply blanch them briefly, or make them into the Korean-influenced ramen condiment known as *moyashi namuru*.

14. CABBAGE
Use a tender variety such as hispi or flat cabbage. Boil for a minute so it retains its texture. An essential component of Jirō-style, but also at home in tonkotsu and miso ramen.

15. BABY BOK CHOY AND CHINESE LEAF
Almost exclusively found in Chinese-style soups, particularly tantanmen. Chinese leaf (Napa cabbage) is my preference, as its slurps better and holds broth beautifully. Bok choy looks better, but it's not as easy to eat.

16. SPINACH
Use large, whole-leaf spinach, never baby. Keep the stems together while cooking so they can be aligned after draining and cut into neat bundles. Shock in iced water after blanching and gently squeeze dry. Mainly found in shōyu soups but also nice in spicy ramen.

17. MENMA
Seasoned bamboo shoots are perhaps the most ubiquitous ramen topping besides spring onions (scallions). Chinese versions are not the same, so make sure you use a Japanese brand or go with the recipe on page 150.

18. GINGER (GRATED)
Adds a delicious, uplifting warmth to bowls; especially good with chicken. Ensure you use a fine, sharp grater to eliminate tough fibres in the ginger.

19. BENI SHŌGA
Red pickled ginger, sharp, sweet and artificially coloured. Good with tonkotsu. Sushi ginger is not an acceptable substitute.

→

20. RAW SHALLOTS (DICED)
Add sparks of sharp sweetness, nice with fish-forward bowls. Red onions work, as well, but they are more intense.

21. FRIED SHALLOTS OR GARLIC
Slice them thinly and start cooking in cold oil, slowly raising the temperature so they cook off all their moisture before they colour. Remove with a slotted spoon when nicely browned and drain on paper towels. Crispy when dry, but silky and sweet when bathed in broth.

22. CHOPPED OR MINCED GARLIC
Upfront and intense; only for strongly flavoured bowls. Chopping garlic a day ahead of serving will dampen its harsh raw flavour. Minced garlic may turn bluish-green due to enzyme activity.

23. SPICY PICKLED MUSTARD GREENS
Karashi takana-zuke in Japanese. A must with Hakata and Kumamoto ramen. Sour, spicy and salty, with background notes of mustard and sesame.

24. SLICED CITRUS (LIME, LEMON OR SIMILAR)
Inspired by older Japanese noodle traditions, slices of sharp citrus may be added to bowls to gently infuse and provide an uplifting aroma. Not intended to be eaten.

25. TOMATOES (FRESH OR ROASTED)
Sliced or chopped fresh tomatoes add a pleasant acidity and extra umami. Roasted ones add sweetness, have a luscious juicy mouthfeel and carry broth well. Great with shōyu or miso in particular.

26. CORN
Common in Hokkaido styles such as Sapporo miso or Hakodate shio. Delicious, but does not slurp well. Often found with butter.

27. CORIANDER (CILANTRO)
Rare in most styles, but often found on tantanmen. Its heady aroma helps freshen up oily soups and tastes great with chilli.

28. BASIL
Used primarily in tomato-based ramen but also works well with miso as well as chicken paitan. Don't use too much or it will overpower the bowl.

具材

野菜と挽肉の炒め
Yasai to Hikiniku no Itame

Stir-Fried Mince and Vegetables

Sapporo-style miso ramen is often topped with a wok-fried mixture of minced (ground) pork and various vegetables, typically made up mostly of bean sprouts, cabbage and onion, but it may also contain things like carrots, red (bell) peppers and kikurage. Chanpon, from Nagasaki, is also topped with a similar kind of stir-fry, but with a generous amount of shellfish and fish cakes instead of the more economical pork mince (ground pork). In Sapporo, the stir-fry is often further integrated into the bowl by briefly boiling in the soup and tare, which seasons and tenderises the veg and transfers a bit of fresh, sweet flavour to the soup.

Makes enough for 4 bowls

1 tablespoon lard or vegetable oil

½ onion, thinly sliced

100 g (3.5 oz) minced (ground) meat (pork is typical but chicken, turkey or vegan mince work, too)

¼ hispi (pointed) or flat cabbage, cored and coarsely chopped

½ small carrot, cut into planks about 3 mm (0.1 in) thick

a big handful of bean sprouts

a few mangetout (snow peas)

¼ red (bell) pepper, thinly sliced

a small pinch of salt and/or MSG (optional)

1 teaspoon sesame oil, or aroma oil of your choice

Have all of your veg prepped and ready to go, because the cooking here should be very quick. In a wok or frying pan, heat the lard or oil over a high heat and add the onion and mince and stir-fry for a couple minutes, then add the cabbage and carrot and continue to stir-fry for 2–3 minutes until everything is wilted but still crunchy. Add the bean sprouts and mangetout and continue to stir-fry for another 2–3 minutes, then add the pepper and salt and/or MSG (use this sparingly, or not at all, if you're going to boil the mixture in seasoned soup). Stir-fry for a further 2 minutes or so, then remove from the heat and stir in the sesame or aroma oil. If you like, you can now add broth and tare to the wok and bring it to the boil, immediately before cooking the noodles and plating the ramen.

具材

Menma

Menma are seasoned bamboo shoots which have undergone a lengthy process of dehydrating, salting, fermenting and finally cooking and/or marinating in a flavourful sauce. They are different from ordinary tinned bamboo shoots, with a wiry, crisp texture and a sweet-salty-funky flavour. Until recently, I never saw the point in making them myself, because off-the-shelf menma was readily available and perfectly tasty. However, in the past year or so there's been a strange menma shortage in the UK, and what is available is either not very good, quite expensive, or both. So I had a go at making my own from a packet of brined Chinese bamboo, and it was surprisingly easy and delicious. And, it's customisable. Use this recipe as a jumping off point, and adjust the seasonings to suit your palate or your ramen.

Makes ≈150 g (5.3 oz) (enough for 5 or 6 bowls of ramen)

200–250 g (7–8.8 oz) bamboo shoots (drained weight), from a tin or packet

1 tablespoon sesame oil

2 tablespoons sake

2 tablespoons shōyu

1 tablespoon mirin

1 teaspoon chicken stock powder, dashi powder, MSG or a mix of any or all of the three

a few drops chilli oil and/or a pinch of chilli (hot pepper) flakes

¼ teaspoon rice vinegar

water, as needed

Preheat the oven to 130°C fan (300°F), then drain the bamboo shoots. I prefer Chinese varieties which are packed in a citric acid brine rather than a salt brine, but either will work. Some bamboo shoots smell a bit like pee and/or are very salty. If either of these apply to your bamboo, blanch them in boiling water for a minute to remove some of the funk or the salt, then proceed with the recipe.

Lay the bamboo out on a baking sheet, or better yet, on a wire rack set over a baking sheet, in a single layer if possible (don't worry if they overlap a bit). Dehydrate these in the oven for about 1 hour 30 minutes, turning and tossing them once or twice during that time to dry more evenly. They might take on some colour – this is no bad thing.

Tip the dehydrated bamboo into a frying pan with the sesame oil and set over a medium-high heat. Stir-fry for 5–6 minutes until the bamboo lightly browns, then tip in all of the remaining seasonings except the vinegar, with just enough water to come up just below the surface of the bamboo. Stir well and reduce the heat to medium, then braise until the liquid reduces to a very thick glaze, about 10 minutes, stirring frequently. Once the bamboo have absorbed the seasoning and the pan is almost totally dry, remove from the heat and stir in the vinegar. Keep in a jar in the refrigerator for up to a week.

NOTE

At the restaurant we made super-spicy menma with Scotch bonnets from Brixton Market puréed into the brine. You can do the same with this recipe if you like; just add about 10–15 g (0.35–0.5 oz) Scotch bonnets, finely chopped, to the seasoning liquid as the menma cook.

具材

6

FULL RAMEN

完全なラーメン

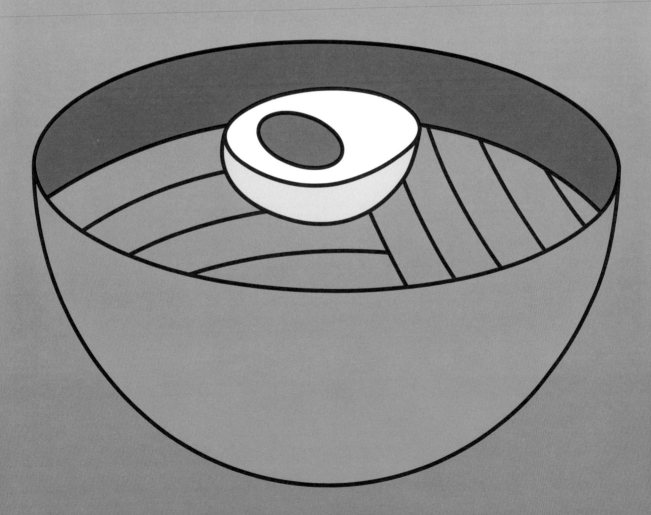

Here we are: time to make ramen! You've got your broth, your tare, your noodles, your oil and your toppings ready to go. Or maybe you don't – that's okay, too, because this chapter also includes 'self-contained' ramen recipes, some of which don't require you to make separate oils or tares or chāshū because they are all produced as part of the same cooking process. But whatever ramen you're making, get yourself set up properly before you start cooking. Here's what you'll need:

1
Your broth, piping hot but not boiling

2
Your noodles, tare, aroma oil and toppings, all of which should be at room temperature or warmer

3
Ladles or some other way of accurately dosing broth and tare

7
Chopsticks, soup spoons and condiments or side dishes already on the table (so you can eat the ramen as soon as it's ready)

8
Drinks! Water, beer or iced barley tea or oolong are typical

4
Bowls, ideally kept warm in a low oven

5
A big pot of water for boiling noodles, and noodle baskets or something else for pulling them out of the water and draining

6
Cooking chopsticks, tongs and tasting spoons

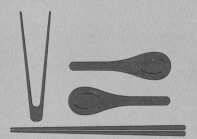

Most ramen is cooked and assembled the same way: add tare to bowl, cook noodles, ladle broth into bowl as the noodles are cooking, drain noodles, carefully tip noodles into broth, stir or fold noodles, add the toppings. Oil can be added at the beginning or end, depending on how you want it to look and mix with the rest of the soup. However, some ramen is constructed a bit differently – I have flagged this in individual recipes and provided a method.

If you are serving other people, gather them to the table before you drop in the noodles, to make sure the ramen isn't sitting around before they tuck in. And then it's your turn. Dish up your ramen, just how you like it. Plate it just so. Take a moment to enjoy the way it looks, the way it smells. Take a picture. Then tuck in. Relax, slurp, repeat. *Gochisō sama deshita* and *otsukare sama deshita*. You did it. And you earned it!

熊本風焦がしニンニク豚骨ラーメン　Garlic Tonkotsu Ramen

Kumamoto Fū Kogashi Ninniku Tonkotsu Ramen

This is my death-row ramen, the kind that got me hooked on ramen and had me coming back countless times as a young man. To accent and perfume the rich porkiness of the broth, there are two forms of garlic: burnt garlic oil and fried garlic chips. This combination of tonkotsu and toasted garlic – along with thin, hard noodles and kikurage – is a classic feature of Kumamoto ramen, the ramen I'd want as my last meal. A bowl of this and a few whiskies and I'd be on my way.

BROTH
Tonkotsu

TARE
Any shio
Shōyu-Shio Hybrid

NOODLES
Hard and Thin

OILS
Black Māyu

TOPPINGS
Fried garlic
'Broasted' Pork Belly
 Chāshū
Kikurage
Spring onions
 (scallions)

OPTIONAL TOPPINGS
Beni shōga
Spicy pickled
 mustard greens
Sesame seeds
'Nduja
(Spicy) Nikumiso
Cabbage
Ajitama (ramen egg)

Follow the method on page 155.

札幌風味噌ラーメン　Miso Ramen

Sapporo Fū Miso Ramen

The more ramen I eat, the more I'm drawn to miso ramen. Thanks to its complex tare and the many textures found in its stir-fried veg topping, it's just so damn interesting. Cooking and plating are a little different for this one, so make sure you read the method below.

BROTH
Any will do, but
 I prefer a paitan

TARE
Any miso

NOODLES
Springy-Chewy

OILS
Lard
Allium and Ginger
 Schmaltz
Garlic Sesame
Chilli

TOPPINGS
Stir-Fried Mince
 and Vegetables
Menma
Shredded spring
 onions (scallions)
 or leeks

OPTIONAL TOPPINGS
Chāshū (any kind)
Corn
Butter
Chilli threads
Chilli oil
Spinach or wakame
Parmesan
Beni shōga
Sesame seeds
Ajitama (ramen egg)

You can build this bowl as you would any other ramen, but I think it's tastier the way many shops in Sapporo do it, which is to combine everything in a wok and then transfer it to the bowl. Start with the stir-fry (page 148) and when it's done, stir in the tare, then the broth. Whisk to combine and bring to the boil. Meanwhile, cook the noodles in a separate pot of boiling water, and when they're done, drain well and tip them into bowls. Pour the broth from the wok over the noodles along with the stir-fried and boiled veg, keeping the veg on top of the noodles as you portion them out. The fat can either be added to the bowl or to the wok; if you add it to the wok it will become emulsified with the broth upon boiling, but it will taste the same. If topping with butter and corn, add cold butter at the last minute, just before serving.

Garlic Tonkotsu Ramen

完全なラーメン

Miso Ramen

Full Ramen

Old-School Shōyu Ramen

完全なラーメン

懐古風東京醤油 ラーメン

Kaikofū Tokyo Shōyu Ramen

Old-School Shōyu Ramen

This is the iconic, Tokyo-style ramen also known by its more antiquated name, *Chūka soba*, which features a clean, clear broth boldly seasoned with soy sauce and chewy, medium-thick noodles that can range from straight to quite curly. The soup tends to be fishy with niboshi and/or katsuobushi and there should be a generous amount of chicken fat or lard on top. To me, this bowl is all about complexity and balance – there are flavours both strong and subtle here and it takes a seasoned palate to bring them all together. It's a tricky one to get right, but once you do, your reward is a ramen with tremendous depth and complexity.

BROTH
Any chintan

TARE
Any shōyu

NOODLES
Go-To

OILS
Schmaltz
Lard
Allium and Ginger
 Schmaltz and/or
 Garlic Sesame

TOPPINGS
Broth-Boiled Pork
 Shoulder Chāshū
Spring onions
 (scallions) or leeks
Spinach
Narutomaki
Menma

OPTIONAL TOPPINGS
Bean sprouts
Ajitama (ramen egg)

Follow the method on page 155.

東京モーダンラーメン

Tokyo Mōdan Ramen

'Tokyo Modern' Ramen

This was our primary ramen at Nanban's second site, a more 'mainstream' offering for a more mainstream location, near Covent Garden. The name was chosen because it synthesises a variety of ramen styles which have either originated or become popular in Tokyo. It is a shōyu chicken paitan, with fish powder, nori oil, fried shallots and chicken chāshū. If your idea of comfort food involves both roast chicken and katsuo dashi, you'll probably dig this bowl.

BROTH
Chicken Paitan

TARE
Any shōyu (ideally Stout
 and Tomato)

NOODLES
Go-To
Springy-Chewy

OILS
Nori

TOPPINGS
Any chicken chāshū
Spring onions (scallions)
Menma
Fried shallots
Seafood Sawdust
Ajitama (ramen egg)
Bean sprouts

OPTIONAL TOPPINGS
Chilli oil
Shiitake mushrooms

Follow the method on page 155.

'Tokyo Modern' Ramen

完全なラーメン

懐古風函館
塩ラーメン

Kaikofū Hakodate Shio Ramen

Old-School Shio Ramen

Many ramen styles are known for their intensity. Tonkotsu, Sapporo miso, curry ramen, tantanmen and Jirō are all dialled way up in terms of flavour, fat and salt. To some, that's what ramen's all about – sensory extremes, bowls of food that light up your taste buds like a pinball machine and land like a gut punch. I do love bowls like these, but I have come to appreciate the humble shio ramen. It took me a while to understand this style, which is often quite plain and austere. But then I realised that's the point: the purity of flavour and gentleness of its impact is meant to soothe, not excite. After all, it's chicken noodle soup – a balm, a salve, something to warm you up on a biting cold day or coddle you when you're under the weather. One thing I particularly came to enjoy about shio ramen is how its clean, mellow flavour allows the noodles themselves to shine. So choose good ones and cook them well.

BROTH
Any chintan

TARE
Any shio

NOODLES
Go-To
Springy-Chewy
Soba-Ramen Hybrid

OILS
Schmaltz
Lard
Allium and Ginger
 Schmaltz

TOPPINGS
Broth-Boiled Pork
 Shoulder Chāshū
Spring onions
 (scallions) and/or
 chives
Menma

OPTIONAL TOPPINGS
Grated ginger
Buttered corn
Ramen Pepper
Ajitama
 (ramen egg)
Onsen egg
Cress
Fu (dried
 wheat gluten)

Follow the method on page 155.

完全なラーメン

室蘭風カレー
ラーメン

Muroran Fū Karē Ramen

Curry Ramen

I am currently studying the local cuisines of Hokkaido for another book, and on research trips there I have eaten *many* outstandingly delicious things. But if asked to choose a favourite, it would have to be the curry ramen from Aji no Daiō in the industrial city of Muroran. I think about this ramen every day. This recipe is as close as I've been able to get to recreating it, but I am determined to get closer. It's nice to have a ramen dream to chase, even if it may be unattainable. *Perfect ramen is the friend of good ramen.*

BROTH
Any except
  vegetable paitan

TARE
Curry, plus Stout and
  Tomato Shōyu or
  any miso

NOODLES
Spring-Chewy –
  make sure you
  temomi them very
  well so they have
  a very tight curl

OILS
Lard

TOPPINGS
Spring onions
  (scallions)
Wakame
Broth-Boiled Pork
  Shoulder Chāshū
Bean sprouts
Chilli (hot pepper)
  flakes, chilli oil or
  shichimi (optional)

First, make the curry broth by combining the broth with the curry tare in a saucepan and bringing them to the boil. Whisk well or use a stick blender to ensure the tare is well mixed. Keep at a low boil for 6–7 minutes to cook out the spices and make them less grainy. During this time the soup may reduce slightly, so add a little water as necessary to maintain the same volume (the soup should be very thick, but not so much that it starts to feel like a sauce). Once the curry has been cooked through, add the shoyu or miso tare and keep at a bare simmer.

When the broth is well cooked and the right consistency, get all your toppings ready and put the lard in the bottom of your bowls. Blanch the spring onions and wakame, cook the noodles and ladle the soup into each bowl. Tip in the noodles and top with the spring onions, wakame, chāshū, bean sprouts and chilli (if using).

つけ麺
Tsukemen

Tsukemen

It's odd writing a recipe for tsukemen because, like ramen itself, it's more a category of dishes rather than a single dish. It's essentially ramen, reformatted – the noodles, and often some or all of the toppings, are served separately from the broth. Everything, therefore, is kept at its optimum texture and temperature until it all comes together in your mouth. Generally, the broth has to be thick and highly seasoned for this to work – typically based on a tonkotsu or otherwise rich broth, further thickened with some kind of fish powder and bolstered by a potent shōyu tare.

This recipe is a sort of synthesis of three of my favourite tsukemen from Tokyo, the 'original' version made at Taishōken and modern versions found at Fūunji and Kissō. The main thing that unites these bowls is their fish-forwardness, being made with generous quantities of gyofun, mostly niboshi. However, the Taishōken version is unique in that it has a subtle but distinctive sweet-and-sour flavour from added vinegar and sugar. Anyway, think of this recipe, and tsukemen generally, as more of a template. All sorts of things work in a tsukemen format; I am especially fond of miso tsukemen, curry tsukemen or ponzu-based tsukemen.

BROTH
Tonkotsu or
Pork and
Chicken Paitan
(See recipe)

TARE
Any shōyu

NOODLES
Thick and Soft
Toasted Sesame

OIL
Allium and Ginger
Schmaltz or lard

TOPPINGS
1–2 slices chāshū
(any kind)
Ajitama
(ramen egg)
Nori
Menma
Spring onions
(scallions)
Seafood Sawdust
(or similar)

Makes 2 servings

Broth and oil

20 g (0.7 oz) niboshi or Seafood Sawdust (page 139)	
500 ml (17 fl oz) Tonkotsu broth (page 27) or Pork and Chicken Paitan (page 34)	
90–120 ml (3–4 fl oz) shōyu tare	
1 teaspoon rice vinegar	
1 teaspoon brown sugar	
2 pinches of shichimi	
4 tablespoons Allium and Ginger Schmaltz (page 92) or lard	

If you're using niboshi, tip them into a saucepan and set over a medium heat. Toast the niboshi for 6–7 minutes until aromatic and lightly browned, then tip out of the pan and leave to cool, then blend them to a powder in a food processor. (If you're using seafood sawdust, you can skip this part.) Reserve 2 small spoonfuls of the fish powder, then add the rest of the fish powder back into the pan along with the broth. Bring to the boil and boil for about 5 minutes to soften the fish powder, then blend using an immersion blender. Add the tare, vinegar, sugar and shichimi, and keep at a low simmer until ready to serve.

Prepare all of the toppings and set aside (reheat them and keep warm, if necessary). Heat the schmaltz in a saucepan until very hot (test this by flicking a few drops of water at it; if it sizzles immediately, it's hot enough). Once everything is ready, cook the noodles according to the guide on page 66, but cook them a minute or so longer than you usually would, because they will firm up quite a bit once chilled. Rinse the cooked noodles in cold water to stop the cooking and remove excess starch, then transfer them to a serving dish or plate. Top the noodles with the egg and nori.

Pour the hot broth into separate bowls, then top with the chāshū, menma and spring onions, followed by the hot schmaltz. Add a small spoonful of seafood sawdust. To eat, dip the cold noodles into the hot broth and slurp. When the noodles are gone, add a little bit of hot water or unseasoned broth to the soup to dilute it and drink it down.

完全なラーメン

Full Ramen

二郎系ラーメン
Jirō-Kei Ramen

Jirō-Style Ramen

The essential ramen blog Ramen Beast has published a wonderful guide and ode to Ramen Jirō, explaining how its excess, its cheap ingredients and its messiness act as a pointed rebuttal to the finesse of the kodawari movement. To me, this makes Jirō a torch-bearer for what ramen has traditionally always been about. Making something special out of nothing special is the beautiful alchemy of ramen. But what is the first comment below the article? 'Jirō is f-ing gross.'

As much as I love Jirō, this commenter is not wrong. Jirō is gross. It's obscene. It's covered in snot-like globs of boiled fat, it's so salty you can feel your veins throbbing after you eat it, it has enough boiled cabbage to supply you with an eternity of farts, and if you order it with minced garlic (which you should), you'll be able to use your own sweat as an aroma oil for another bowl of ramen.

But what exactly is Jirō? On paper, it's pretty simple: an un-emulsified tonkotsu broth; a basic tare which is mostly (or entirely) soy sauce, mirin and MSG; irregularly-shaped, thick, hard, slightly grainy noodles; and toppings of seasoned back fat, a huge pile of boiled cabbage and bean sprouts, thick chunks of shoulder chāshū and (on request) finely chopped raw garlic. In practice, there are countless complexities that go into all of these elements, especially the broth. The go-to guy for Jirō research is Elvin Yung (@shikaku.ramen), who has put together an incredibly detailed breakdown of how Jirō is made, which I encourage you to read.

It's insanely complicated and, really, a lot of it comes down to the chef's taste, intuition and their ability to make minor adjustments on the fly. There is an inherent inconsistency to Jirō, not only from branch to branch but even within the same shop, so it takes a confident and trained palate to ensure it tastes 'right' every time.

Ultimately, I think of Jirō more in terms of the unique sensory experience it provides; it may be best understood by the overall effect it has on you. If it's overwhelming, challenging and excessive, yet hopelessly addictive and irresistible all at once, then you've probably got it right.

By the way, there is some debate as to whether Jirō-inspired bowls that aren't served at actual Jirō shops should be called Jirō-kei (Jirō-style); many ramenheads prefer the more generic terms 'gattsuri-kei' or 'G-kei'. While I completely understand this point and actually kind of agree with it, I use the name 'Jirō-style' here mainly to refer readers back to the style's originator, who deserves to be recognised as such.

BROTH
Tonkotsu
 (see recipe)
 or Vegetable
 Jirō-Style

TARE
Jirō-Style

NOODLES
Wholegrain Jirō-Style

OILS
Seasoned Back Fat

TOPPINGS
Hispi (pointed)
 cabbage (allow
 at least ¼ head
 of cabbage per
 portion)
Bean sprouts (about
 120–150 g (4.2–
 5.3 oz) per portion)
Broth-Boiled Pork
 Shoulder Chāshū
 (allow 200 g/7 oz
 per portion),
 thickly sliced
Minced garlic
 (see recipe)

Prepare the toppings. Garlic should be coarsely minced and you will need at least four cloves per bowl. Do this a few hours ahead of time and, ideally, the day before or the garlic will be very harsh and intense. Allowing the garlic to sit for a day in the refrigerator will let its astringency dissipate and mellow. Coarsely chop the cabbage and cut the chāshū into thick chunks (at least 1 cm/½ in and up to 2 cm/¾ in) thick). Prior to cooking, reheat the chāshū and keep it warm.

Jirō-style soup is a pure tonkotsu, but it is not emulsified, and it is made through a complex double-extraction process called *yobimodoshi*. For a more authentically Jirō soup, you can read up on this online, but it is not practical for home cooks, nor for most professional kitchens, either. For our purposes, a straightforward tonkotsu broth (or the vegetarian version on page 43) will do, but don't blend or boil to re-emulsify it, and lob in some of the seasoned back fat to recreate a Jirō-esque appearance

The tare (page 55) can be constructed in each bowl, but you may want to make it separately so you have extra to marinate the chāshū and drizzle over the toppings (this is called *karame* in Jirō-ese). Once your toppings and broth are ready, bring a pot of water to the boil. Drop in the vegetables and cook for a few minutes until wilted but still firm, then drain them and tip them into the broth to keep hot. Add the noodles to the boiling water and cook until very hard. Pour the broth into each bowl, then drain the noodles and tip them in, and top with a big pile of vegetables. Add a big spoonful each of the seasoned back fat and the minced garlic, then the chāshū. If you like, add more tare to the top of the vegetables.

完全なラーメン

Full Ramen

豚の頭の半分で
作られる豚骨ラーメン

Buta no Atama no Hanbun de Tsukurareru
Tonkotsu Ramen

Half a Pig's Head Ramen

There's good meat in the head. Maybe the best meat, rich and sticky and dense with porky flavour. At the restaurant we had to shorten the boil on our tonkotsu broth because the early starts and late finishes required to get it done were too much to ask of our staff. At that point I rejigged the recipe so we could get the same viscosity and flavour in 10 hours. The most dramatic change to the recipe came in the form of a whole pig's head. Pig's heads are surprisingly cheap and they efficiently added a huge amount of gelatine, fat and flavour to the broth in a relatively short amount of time. The only problem was it seemed like a waste of good meat. This recipe corrects that by rescuing the tastiest part of the head (the jowls) before they're completely obliterated by the boil, tossing them through a simple tare and serving them as chāshū. Like the Whole Chicken Ramen (page 183), it's a delicious, 'self-contained' ramen with maximum flavour and minimum wastage.

BROTH
See recipe

TARE
See recipe

NOODLES
Hard and Thin

OILS
There will be plenty of lard in the broth, but you could also add Allium and Ginger Schmaltz, Black Māyu or Chilli

TOPPINGS
Spring onions (scallions)
Bean sprouts
Beni shōga
'Nduja

OPTIONAL TOPPINGS
Pickled mustard greens
Black pepper or Ramen Pepper

Makes 8 servings

Broth

Broth
½ pig's head
2 leeks, coarsely chopped
100 g (3.5 oz) ginger, thinly sliced
4 garlic bulbs, halved
1 head celery, coarsely chopped
1 apple, halved
2 tablespoons peppercorns (either white or black are fine)
≈4 litres (135 fl oz) water
4 tablespoons mirin
4 tablespoons sake
1 tablespoon MSG
120 ml (4 fl oz) usukuchi soy sauce
80 g (2.8 oz) red miso
40 g (1.4 oz) white miso
salt, to taste

To make the broth, blanch and wash the half pig's head according to the guide on page 25 to remove the blood and gunk. Because the head is so large, let it blanch for longer than usual (about 15 minutes) in order to extract all of the blood.

Divide all of the vegetables into two containers, so you have roughly the same amount of each vegetable in each one. Combine one half of the veg with the blanched pig's head and the peppercorns in a stockpot and add enough water to cover. Bring to the boil and sustain for 3 hours, topping up the water periodically to maintain the water level.

At this point, use strong tongs or a spider to remove the pig's head from the broth and reduce the heat on the broth to a low simmer. Leave the head to cool. When it is cool enough to handle, remove the cheeks from the head. You should be able to simply pull the meat away from the bone, but if it is still a bit tough, use a boning knife to carve it off. Return the rest of the head to the pan and continue to boil for another 3 hours. At the final hour, add the remaining vegetables to the broth.

→

Chāshū

1½ teaspoons sesame oil
4 tablespoons shōyu
4 tablespoons Shaoxing wine or medium sherry
2 tablespoons light brown sugar
½ teaspoon smoked paprika
1 tablespoon gochujang
broth-braised pig cheeks (see recipe)

Meanwhile, prepare the chāshū. Whisk together all of the ingredients, except the cheeks, and bring to the boil in a small saucepan or in the microwave to cook off the alcohol in the Shaoxing wine. Leave to cool slightly, then toss the cheeks in the liquid and leave to marinate until ready to serve.

After the second half of the boil is finished, remove the skull from the broth and discard, then strain according to the guide on page 26. Measure the broth and top up with water to make 2.4 litres (81 fl oz). Rinse out the stockpot, then add the mirin, sake and MSG. Bring to the boil, then add the soy sauce and miso and mix well, ensuring there are no lumps of miso. Return the broth to the stockpot and stir, then bring to a simmer. Taste and adjust seasoning as necessary with salt. If you like, emulsify the broth with a stick blender.

Prepare or reheat the toppings as needed and set aside. Once everything is ready, cook the noodles and plate the ramen according to the guide on page 155. Add the chāshū and toppings however you like.

NOTE
Pig's heads are delicious but they have a very pungent aroma – too pungent for most. This recipe has additions of aromatic vegetables in two stages, first to flavour the meat used as chāshū and later to infuse into the broth itself.

坦々麺
Tantanmen

Tantanmen probably doesn't need an introduction, but for the uninitiated, it is a Japanese interpretation of Sichuanese dan dan noodles, in which the classic sesame- and chilli-based sauce is transformed into a rich broth. I think the key to tantanmen is not to hold back with both the tantan tare and the chilli oil. I also highly recommend using the Mala Mix (page 138) to ramp up aroma and add a tongue-tingling buzz of Sichuan peppercorns.

BROTH
Any paitan

TARE
Tantan, plus any
  shio or miso

NOODLES
Go-to
Thick and Soft
Toasted Sesame
Wholegrain
  Jirō-Style
Shop-bought/instant

OILS
Chilli
Garlic Sesame and/
  or Black Pepper
Bacon

TOPPINGS
(Spicy) Nikumiso
Coriander (cilantro)
  leaves
Mala Mix, to taste
Spring onions
  (scallions),
  finely sliced
Sesame seeds

OPTIONAL TOPPINGS
'Broasted' Chāshū or
  Lapsang Souchong-
  Brined Pork or
  Chicken Chāshū
Menma
Chinese leaf or baby
  bok choy, blanched
Fried garlic
Grated Parmesan

Prepare all of the toppings and set aside (keep them warm if necessary) until ready to cook the noodles. Use a whisk to blend the two tare together before adding the broth and whisking again to combine. Top with the spicy nikumiso and many spoonfuls of chilli oil (and/or the other recommended oils), followed by the remaining toppings. Once everything is ready, cook the noodles and plate the ramen according to the guide on page 155.

フル・イングリッシュ・ブレックファスト風担々麺

Furu Ingurisshu Burekkufasuto Fū Tantanmen

Full English Tantanmen

The full English breakfast and ramen occupy similar gastronomic spaces in their respective cultures. They're both first and foremost a working-class pork and carb delivery mechanism, engineered to maximise the satiety-to-cost ratio. However, both can be regionalised, fussed over and gussied up (to some extent), making them something all strata of society can get behind. They are democratic foods, but more importantly, they are both perfect for a hangover.

BROTH
Any paitan

TARE
Tantan plus any shio,
  miso or Stout
  and Tomato Shōyu

NOODLES
Go-to, Egg,
  Thick and Soft
Toasted Sesame
Wholegrain Jirō-Style
Shop-bought/instant

OILS
Chilli
Garlic Sesame
Black Pepper Bacon

TOPPINGS
Breakfast Soboro
  (see recipe)
2 rashers back
  bacon, grilled
  (broiled)
2 eggs, fried
  in butter
2 potato smiles or
  hash browns (or
  similar), cooked
  according to the
  packet instructions
1 handful coriander
  (cilantro) leaves
Mala Mix, to taste
Spring onions
  (scallions),
  finely sliced
Sesame seeds
Black Pepper Bacon

OPTIONAL TOPPINGS
Menma
Fried garlic

Serves 2

Breakfast soboro

2 rashers streaky bacon,
cut into lardons

2 tablespoons chilli oil

½ onion, finely diced

2 garlic cloves, finely chopped

50 g (1.75 oz) button mushrooms
(or similar), finely diced

100 g (3.5 oz) English sausage
meat, or a mix of sausage and
black pudding, white pudding
or haggis

4 tablespoons baked beans

2 tinned peeled plum tomatoes,
coarsely chopped

shōyu, miso and/or brown sauce,
to taste

Prepare all of the toppings and set aside (keep them warm if necessary) until ready to cook the noodles.

To make the soboro, heat the bacon and chilli oil together in a frying pan over a medium heat. When the bacon is no longer raw and beginning to brown, add the onion and sauté for 4–5 minutes to soften. Add the garlic, mushrooms and sausage meat, then continue to sauté for another 8–10 minutes, breaking up the meat as you go to make a crumbled texture. Add the baked beans and tomatoes and continue to cook until the liquid evaporates, about 3 minutes. Stir well and taste the mixture, then add shōyu, miso and/or brown sauce to taste (bear in mind the rest of the dish will be quite salty so don't overdo it).

Once everything is ready, cook the noodles and plate the ramen according to the guide on page 155. Top with the soboro first, followed by the back bacon, fried eggs, potato smiles and then all of the remaining toppings.

完全なラーメン

ピザラーメン
Piza Ramen

Pizza Ramen

It's pizza. It's ramen. I probably don't need to draw you a diagram to explain how delicious this is. While it may sound unforgivably silly, there is some precedent for it. First, in the many tomato ramen that have been around in Japan for years and, more recently, actual pizza-inspired bowls such as the famous pizza-soba at Ajito Ism in Tokyo.

BROTH
Any chintan
Mushroom Dashi

TARE
Miso
Stout and Tomato

NOODLES
Go-To
Springy-Chewy

OILS
Olive oil
 (see recipe)

TOPPINGS
Grated mozzarella
Grated Parmesan
Pizza soboro
 (see recipe)
Crispy pepperoni
 (see recipe)
Pickled guindilla
 peppers (or similar),
 thinly sliced

OPTIONAL TOPPINGS
Garlic pizza crust
 (see recipe)
Chilli (hot pepper)
 flakes
Fresh basil

Serves 2

Garlic pizza crusts (optional)

90 ml (6 tablespoons)
lukewarm water

½ teaspoon dry yeast

1 teaspoon olive oil

140 g (5 oz) plain (all-purpose) flour,
plus extra for dusting

1 teaspoon sugar

¼ teaspoon salt

polenta (cornmeal), for dusting

garlic cloves, as needed

melted unsalted butter, as needed

dried oregano, as needed

Pizza sauce

1 onion, finely diced

60 ml (4 tablespoons) olive oil

10 garlic cloves, finely chopped

140 g (5 oz) tomato purée (paste)

1 tablespoon dried oregano

1.6 kg (3 lb 8 oz) tinned tomatoes
(peeled whole tomatoes or pulp
work best – not chopped)

20 grinds black pepper

50 g (1.75 oz) basil,
roughly chopped

1 teaspoon sugar

½ teaspoon salt

¼ teaspoon MSG

30 g (1 oz) ketchup

Pizza soboro

40 g (1.4 oz) pepperoni, sliced

30 g (1 oz) green olives, sliced

50 g (1.75 oz) tinned mushrooms,
sliced

200 g (7 oz) Sicilian fennel
sausage meat

If making the garlic pizza crusts, whisk together the water, yeast and olive oil until the yeast dissolves. Combine the flour, sugar and salt in a separate bowl, then add the wet mix to the dry mix. Knead for a few minutes, then leave to prove for about an hour, or overnight in the refrigerator. Using plenty of extra flour and polenta, roll the dough out very thinly. Cook the dough until crisp on the bottom in either a very, very hot oven or in a large, flat frying pan. Rub with garlic and brush with melted butter. Before serving, re-crisp in the oven and garnish with dried oregano. Cut into squares to serve.

For the sauce, fry the onion in the olive oil over a medium heat until soft and translucent, then add the garlic and continue to cook until the onion browns very lightly. Add the tomato purée and oregano and stir through, then add the tinned tomatoes and black pepper. Simmer for 4 hours, then add the basil, sugar, salt, MSG and ketchup. Blend with an immersion blender, but not too much – it should have some texture rather than being totally smooth.

To make the soboro, fry the pepperoni in a dry frying pan over a medium heat until crisp, then remove from the pan and drain. Add the remaining ingredients and sauté, breaking up the sausage into crumbles, for about 10 minutes until the meat is cooked through and browned all over.

Have all the toppings prepared and kept warm before cooking the noodles. To make the ramen, put 3–4 tablespoons of tare in each bowl, then add 200 ml (6.75 fl oz) broth and 100 ml (3.5 fl oz) pasta sauce and whisk well to combine. Cook and drain the noodles, then tip into the broth and top with the grated cheeses, soboro, pepperoni, pickled peppers and, if you fancy it, a little pinch of chilli and a few torn basil leaves. Finish with a drizzle of good olive oil and serve the pizza crusts on the side.

NOTE
The sauce recipe makes far more than you'll need for a few bowls of ramen, but this is by design, because it's a delicious sauce. Use it for actual pizza (duh) or as a dip for mozzarella sticks!

完全なラーメン

ウィスコンシン州産 ビールとチーズ ラーメン
Wisukonshin-Shū San Bīru to Chīzu Ramen

Wisconsin Beer and Cheese Ramen

Whenever I think about the kind of ramen I might make to express my own sense of regional identity, inevitably, I think of cheese – you can take the boy out of Wisconsin, but you can't take Wisconsin out of the boy. And while cheesy ramen does exist, I never thought a ramen where cheese was the entire foundation of the soup and not just a topping would be very delicious, or even doable. There's a limit to how far you can push the viscosity of ramen broth, beyond which it becomes like a bowl of pasta in too much sauce (see also: Pizza Ramen (page 178) and Lazy Goat Ragù-Men (page 197)).

Then I remembered beer and cheese soup, an icon of Wisconsin cuisine, which I remember mainly from Polaris, the revolving restaurant on top of the Hilton in downtown Milwaukee, where we'd go for special occasions, like my dad's birthday. The restaurant offered striking views of ... well, mostly nothing, since Milwaukee is flanked on one side by a vast, dark lake and on all the remaining sides by sleepy suburbs and even sleepier farmland. But they also offered this soup – essentially a delicious, rich-but-not-too-rich, beery-but-not-too-beery thinned-out fondue, scented with garlic and served with sourdough croutons. It is Wisconsin, distilled. And it turns out it makes a pretty great ramen.

BROTH
See recipe

TARE
See recipe

NOODLES
Go-To

OILS
Black Pepper
Bacon and/or
Chilli

TOPPINGS
1–2 slices
mortadella
Blanched spinach
Chives, finely
chopped
Fried shallots
Finely grated
Parmesan
2 pieces of
sourdough toast,
lightly buttered
and rubbed with
a garlic clove

OPTIONAL TOPPINGS
Black pepper

Makes 2 servings

Soup

600 ml (20 fl oz) Vegetable Chintan (page 37), Roast Pork and Chicken Chintan (page 32), or Mushroom Dashi (page 42)	
50 ml (1.7 fl oz) Belgian ale	
1 tablespoon nutritional yeast flakes	
1 big pinch of nutmeg	
1 small pinch of ground white pepper	
100 ml (3.5 fl oz) evaporated milk	
90 g (3.2 oz) Miso Tare (page 60) or 60–70 g (2–2.5 oz) miso	
70 g (2.5 oz) mature Cheddar, grated	
30 g (1 oz) Gruyère, grated	
20 g (0.7 oz) Edam, mozzarella, or similar, grated	

Prepare all of the toppings and set aside (keep them warm if necessary) until ready to cook the noodles.

To make the soup, combine the broth, ale, yeast flakes, nutmeg and pepper and bring to the boil. Reduce the heat to a simmer and add the evaporated milk and tare, then add the cheeses, stirring with a spatula as you drop them in. Once the cheeses are incorporated, remove from the heat and blend until smooth with an immersion blender. Return to a low heat while you finish the dish, scraping the sides of the pan periodically with a spatula to release any stuck cheese. (Don't let the broth boil at this point or it may become grainy.)

Once everything is ready, cook the noodles and plate the ramen according to the guide on page 155. Top with the mortadella and spinach first, followed by the remaining toppings, with the toast served on the side.

完全なラーメン

Wスープラーメン
W Sūpu Ramen

Double Soup Ramen

'Double soup' is a relatively recent innovation in ramen, in which two separate broths are made and then combined in a bowl. Different methods of broth-making are better for different ingredients, so if you want to get (for example) strong, rich chicken flavours as well as delicate fish and seaweed flavours into a soup, it's best to cook them separately. This produces soups that are complex and balanced, and typically occupy a nice midway point between heavy paitan and light chintan. It's a fun technique to play around with, so if you have a few broths in the refrigerator or freezer, see what happens when you mix them up. By the way, 'triple soup' is a thing, too, so don't stop at two!

BROTH
Any paitan, plus any dashi or chintan

TARE
Any, but avoid miso as it will overpower the broth

NOODLES
Depends on the soup combination, but try Go-To or Soba-Ramen Hybrid first

OILS
Depends on the soup, but nothing too strong

TOPPINGS
Smoked Chāshū
Spring onions (scallions)
Menma
Bean sprouts

OPTIONAL TOPPINGS
Nori
Narutomaki
Ajitama (ramen egg)
Fried shallots
Seafood Sawdust

Follow the method on page 155. You can either combine the two broths directly in each bowl, or in a saucepan prior to serving.

Many shops in Japan, especially those specialising in shōyu or shio ramen, make their broth from whole chickens, typically simmered gently to minimise loss of aroma and maximise clarity. While this does make a lovely broth, I never made mine this way because I always thought it seems like a waste – what do I do with all that chicken once the broth is made?

The answer is to eat it – duh! It will still be tasty as long it's seasoned well. Like the Half a Pig's Head Ramen (page 173), this is a 'self-contained' ramen recipe in that the soup, chāshū and oil are all derived from the same process.

The broth recipe here is adapted from Ivan Orkin's, but his uses nothing other than chicken. I can't resist leek and ginger with chicken, but feel free to leave them out if you prefer, especially if you are using really good-quality chicken.

BROTH
See recipe

TARE
See recipe

NOODLES
Go-To, Shop-bought/instant, Springy-Chewy, Soba-Ramen Hybrid, Egg

OILS
See Note, below

TOPPINGS
Spring onions (scallions)
Fried shallots
Ajitama (ramen egg) or Onsen Egg

OPTIONAL TOPPINGS
Seafood Sawdust
Ramen Pepper
Nori
Grated ginger

**Makes 8 servings
(plus extra chicken)**

Broth

1 whole chicken (about 1.5 kg/ 3 lb 5 oz)	
≈3.5 litres (118 fl oz) water	
½ leek, roughly chopped	
10 g (0.35 oz) kombu	
40 g (1.4 oz) fresh ginger root, thinly sliced	
2 tablespoons usukuchi soy sauce	
1 tablespoon (15 g/0.5 oz) salt	
1 teaspoon (2 g/0.1 oz) dashi powder	
½ teaspoon MSG	

Chāshū

3 tablespoons shōyu	
2 tablespoons oyster sauce	
1 tablespoon honey	
1½ teaspoons sesame oil	

To make the broth, place the chicken in a pot and cover with the water. Set over a medium-high heat and bring to a low boil, skimming the scum that forms on the surface regularly. Keep boiling for about 15 minutes, collecting scum frequently, then reduce the heat to between 85–90°C (185–194°F). Use a thermometer for this. Place a drop lid (page 42) on the chicken and hold the temperature at that range for 4 hours. About 2 hours in, press down on the chicken with a wooden spoon or similar, so that it starts to split apart. Do this again after another 2 hours.

After a total of 4 hours, add the leek, kombu and ginger and continue to cook at the same temperature for another hour. Remove from the heat, strain and measure the liquid (save the chicken!). The yield should be 2.4 litres (81 fl oz), so top up (or reduce) the liquid as needed. Add all the seasonings, stir well and refrigerate until needed.

When the chicken is cool enough to handle, pull the meat off the bones and divide the meat in half – you'll only need half to make eight bowls of ramen, so transfer the rest to the refrigerator and save it for something else (it's nice in a salad or a quesadilla). With the remaining half, cut or shred the meat into bite-sized pieces. Stir together the chāshū seasonings and then toss the chicken through this marinade. Keep in the refrigerator until ready to use.

Prepare any toppings you'd like to use and set aside. Reheat the chicken in a frying pan, allowing the marinade to caramelise slightly. Bring the broth to a high simmer. Once everything is ready, cook the noodles and plate the ramen according to the guide on page 155. Ensure each bowl has some of the chicken fat from the broth in it. Add the toppings however you like and a lovely colour.

NOTE
Skim the scum that forms at the beginning of the boil, but don't remove the fat that comes up later! This will become the aroma oil for the dish – it has a lot of chickeny flavour

Full Ramen

ターキーラーメン
Tākī Ramen

Turkey Ramen

We made a version of this ramen every Christmas at the restaurant, and I'd have kept it on the menu year-round if I'd thought it would sell – it's that good. Turkey has a bad rap in the UK, but I honestly think that's because nobody cooks it right. If you cook it nicely (as per this recipe), it is a delicious, succulent, flavourful bird. And of course, it makes a great ramen.

BROTH
Chicken Paitan,
 or turkey broth
 (see Note below)

TARE
Any shio

NOODLES
Go-To
Soba-Ramen
 Hybrid
Springy-Chewy

OILS
European Duck
 Fat and/or
 confit turkey oil

TOPPINGS
Confit Turkey Leg
Turkey breast
Turkey crackling
Pickled
 cranberries
Fried shallots
Nira

Serves 8

Pickled cranberries

2.5 cm (1 in) piece fresh ginger, peeled

50–60 g (1.75–2 oz) fresh, frozen
or dried cranberries, halved

60 ml (2 fl oz) beni shōga brine

Turkey breast

1 large turkey breast (about 800 g/
1 lb 12 oz), skin on

1 tablespoon sake

1 tablespoon sugar

salt and white pepper, as needed

Turkey crackling

turkey skin, from the breast
and the confit turkey

salt, as needed

The day before you make the ramen, prepare the pickled cranberries and the turkey breast. For the cranberries, finely grate the ginger and then squeeze the juice from the ginger pulp into a jar or container (discard the solids). Combine with the remaining ingredients, stir well and leave to pickle overnight.

For the turkey breast, remove the skin from the turkey. Massage the sake and sugar into the breast, then season generously with the salt and pepper. Leave in the refrigerator to absorb the seasoning for at least 2 hours. Preheat the oven to 150°C fan (350°F). Lay the turkey breast skin (not the confit skin) out flat on a foil-lined baking tray and transfer to the oven. Place the seasoned breast on another tray and cover with foil, then roast it in the oven as well. Cook the turkey breast until its internal temperature reaches 65°C (150°F) (about 30–40 minutes) then remove from the oven and leave to rest while still covered in foil. Turn the skin over and leave in the oven for another 20–30 minutes until golden brown. Add the confit skin to the same tray, then turn the oven up to 180°C fan (400°F) and roast for a final 10 minutes until completely browned and crisp. Season with salt while still hot.

Slice the breast into thin slices and break the confit leg (page 121) up into irregular bite-size chunks. Reheat both very gently in a few spoonfuls of the confit fat. Once everything is ready, cook the noodles and plate the ramen according to the guide on page 155.

NOTE
Chicken broth works fine for this recipe, but if you are making this from a whole turkey you may as well use the bones for the broth. Simply follow the Chicken Paitan method (page 30) – a hard boil, with aromatic vegetables added towards the end. Because turkey bones are bigger than chicken broth, you may have to boil it about an hour or two longer than you would with chicken to get the same amount of body. But you can also simply add turkey bones to chicken broth and boil it for an hour or so, which will be enough to infuse some flavour if you don't need to extract much gelatine and fat.

完全なラーメン

ナンドスの残り物を使った ラーメン

Nandosu no Nokorimono wo Tsukatta Ramen

Leftover Nando's Ramen

Nando's is a national treasure. Honestly, I don't know anyone who doesn't like Nando's, and what's not to like? I like it in particular because a Nando's order doubles as the basis for a truly great bowl of ramen, provided you get a whole chicken. This may be one of the sillier concepts in this book, but it's also one of the most delicious bowls.

Serves 2

1 whole chicken from Nando's
(any spice level)

1 order of Nando's chicken livers
(at least medium hot)

1 order of Nando's chips

1 order of Nando's corn on the cob

1 tablespoon olive oil or schmaltz

5–6 cherry tomatoes, diced

2 pinches of sesame seeds

≈80–120 g (2.8–4.2 oz) Miso Tare
(page 60) or 60–90 g (2–3.2 oz) miso

2 portions noodles (Go-To
or Springy-Chewy)

small handful coriander
(cilantro) leaves

chilli oil, to taste

2 Ajitama (ramen eggs, page 127)
(optional)

Begin by eating about three-quarters of the chicken, about half of the chicken livers and all but a few of the chips. (Don't eat any of the corn.) Remove the leftover meat from the chicken frame, then place the bones in a saucepan and cover with water. Bring to the boil, then keep at a high simmer with a lid on the pan for 1 hour, topping up the water periodically to maintain a consistent level. Meanwhile, cut the corn kernels from the cob and coarsely chop the livers into a mince-like texture. Heat the olive oil or schmaltz in a frying pan over a medium-high heat and add the livers, corn and tomatoes, then stir-fry for 7–8 minutes until the tomatoes have broken down and the mix is quite dry. Add the sesame seeds and remove from the heat.

When the broth is done, pass it through a sieve and measure it; you should have about 600 ml (20 fl oz), so if it is significantly less than this, top it up with water or reduce it as necessary. Return to the pan and bring to the boil, then reduce the heat to a low simmer and whisk in the miso or miso tare, tasting to adjust the seasoning as you like. Slice the leftover chicken meat into chopstick-friendly slices.

Prepare a separate pan full of boiling water and cook and drain the noodles according to the guide on page 155. Divide the Nando's broth into two bowls, then tip in the noodles and stir through. Top with the liver and corn mixture, the sliced meat, chilli oil, ajitama and coriander leaves.

完全なラーメン

あさり味噌バター
コーンラーメン

Asari Miso Batā Kōn Ramen

Clam Miso Butter Corn Ramen

Clams make delicious dashi (page 38), and if you have delicious dashi, you've got the foundation of a good bowl of ramen. This single-serving, one-pan recipe simply builds upon clams' natural juices to make a quick, tasty ramen out of very little. However, because the broth is so light, this bowl benefits from a thick, absorbent noodle, so the Thick and Soft Noodles (page 78) or Toasted Sesame Noodles (page 84) are ideal, but a chunky shop-bought egg noodle will do, too. In a pinch, you could even use – and I can't believe I'm saying this – *udon*. But that would make it NOT RAMEN and NOT RAMEN is NOT ALLOWED!

Makes 1 serving

20 g (0.7 oz) unsalted butter
1 teaspoon olive oil
1 teaspoon sesame oil
80 g (2.8 oz) tinned sweetcorn (drained weight)
2 spring onions (scallions), white and green parts separated, thinly sliced
½ small mild red chilli, finely chopped
1 tablespoon white wine
1 tablespoon mirin
200–300 g (7–10.6 oz) good-quality clams, cleaned of grit
20 g (0.7 oz) red miso
1 portion noodles
a small handful of spinach or rehydrated wakame
salt, to taste
a few sprigs of flat leaf parsley, roughly chopped

In a medium saucepan, melt the butter over a medium-high heat together with the oils, then add the sweetcorn. Sauté until the corn begins to brown, then add the white part of the spring onion and the chilli. Continue to sauté for a few minutes until the spring onion is softened, then add the wine, mirin and clams. Put a lid on the pan and steam for 3–4 minutes until all of the clams have opened. Remove from the heat and pass everything through a sieve, retaining the liquid. Add enough water to the clam liquid to make 500 ml (17 fl oz), then return the liquid to the pan. Whisk the miso into the clam broth and bring to the boil. Drop the noodles directly into the broth and cook them according to your taste, then switch off the heat, add the spinach or wakame, stir, taste the broth and add salt and/or water as needed. Transfer everything to a bowl, top with the clam and corn mixture, and garnish with the parsley and the green part of the spring onions.

完全なラーメン

'Nothing Special' Ramen

Sometimes the ramen craving strikes and there's no ramen to be found – what do you do? Instant ramen does the job, of course, and some of it is excellent, especially if you're able to add good toppings. But even that is sometimes unavailable. This recipe is designed to tick the proper ramen box from common refrigerator and storecupboard ingredients when you don't have any good broth, nor tare, nor oils, nor nothing!

Makes 1 serving

20 g (0.7 oz) lard
80 g (2.8 oz) minced (ground) pork
2 anchovies
½ onion, thinly sliced
a big handful of bean sprouts
2 garlic cloves, grated
1 tablespoon sesame oil
2 tablespoons red miso
1 tablespoon sugar
1 tablespoon white wine
1 tablespoon tomato purée (paste)
2 tablespoons shōyu
1 tablespoon peanut butter or tahini
a pinch each of white pepper and smoked paprika
500 ml (17 fl oz) water
1 tablespoon grated Parmesan or Cheddar
1 portion shop-bought noodles
a big pinch of sesame seeds
1 spring onion (scallion), thinly sliced
chilli oil, to taste (optional)
salt, to taste

In a wok or medium saucepan, melt the lard over a high heat and add the pork mince, anchovies and onion. Stir-fry for a few minutes, breaking up the anchovies as you go, until the pork is cooked through and the onion has begun to soften. Toss in the bean sprouts and garlic and stir-fry for another 1–2 minutes, then tip everything out into a bowl. Add the sesame oil to the pan and set over a medium heat, then add the miso and sugar and fry it for a few minutes until the aroma becomes rich and caramel-like. Stir in the white wine, tomato purée, shōyu and peanut butter or tahini and cook for another few minutes, then add the pepper, paprika, water and cheese. Bring to the boil, add the noodles and cook them to your liking. Once they're done, taste the broth and add salt or more water as needed – different noodles will absorb different amounts of liquid, so you'll have to adjust for this accordingly. Transfer the broth and noodles to a bowl and top with the stir-fried mince and veg and garnish with the sesame seeds and spring onion. Add as much chilli oil as you like.

トムヤムクンラーメン
Tomuyamukun Ramen

Tom Yum Goong Ramen

Summers at the restaurant were always lousy. Turns out not a lot of people want to sit inside and eat hot soup when it's warm and sunny out. We tried all kinds of things to get the customers in, but nothing ever worked, and the most vexing thing about it was that ramen remained our top seller throughout the summer. I figured, well, the few customers coming through the door were still coming for ramen, so the best we can do is offer a lighter, more summery ramen. And so I took inspiration from the light but exquisitely flavourful Thai soups, namely tom yum. I did some research, asked some of my Thai chef friends for advice and collaborated with my sous chef Sana, who had worked in several Thai restaurants previously. This recipe is a version of what we came up with – a light-bodied ramen with a gorgeous fragrance and lip-smacking tang. 'Asian fusion' is stupid. Unless it isn't. Hopefully this isn't!

Makes 4 servings

2 tablespoons vegetable oil, coconut oil or schmaltz
2 shallots, thinly sliced
1 red chilli, coarsely chopped
10 g (0.35 oz) fresh ginger root
50 g (1.75 oz) galangal
50 g (1.75 oz) lemongrass
10 g (0.35 oz) makrut lime leaves
1.5 litres (51 fl oz) water
6 tablespoons Thai fish sauce
15 g (0.5 oz) palm sugar
juice of 1 lime, plus another lime, quartered
12 large raw prawns (shrimp), shelled and deveined
100 g (3.5 oz) bean sprouts
4 portions noodles (Go-To or Egg work well)
2 spring onions (scallions), shredded
some coriander (cilantro), leaves picked
chilli oil, to taste

Heat the oil in a saucepan over a medium heat and add the shallots and chilli. Sauté for about 8–10 minutes, until the shallots are richly coloured. Meanwhile, bash the ginger, galangal, lemongrass and lime leaves with a blunt object such as a rolling pin or a pestle or the back of a knife to release their oils, then coarsely chop them. Tip them into the oil and sauté for a few minutes, then add the water and bring to a simmer. Simmer for 1 hour, then stir in the fish sauce, palm sugar and lime juice. Remove all of the aromatics with a sieve or slotted spoon and keep the broth warm until ready to use.

Prepare a pot full of boiling water for the noodles and have all of the toppings prepared and ready. Poach the prawns and bean sprouts in the simmering broth for a few minutes, then cook and drain the noodles. Transfer the broth and noodles to bowls, top with the bean sprouts and prawns, then garnish with the spring onions, coriander leaves and chilli oil. Serve with the quartered lime wedges on the side.

完全なラーメン

NOT QUITE RAMEN

The dishes in this chapter sit within the extended family of ramen, but they're different enough to be called something else. This could be because they're soupless, or served cold, or both, but they are still based on alkaline wheat noodles and share many similarities in terms of their overall flavour profile. NOT RAMEN is still NOT ALLOWED, but NOT QUITE RAMEN is PRETTY CLOSE, so I'LL ALLOW IT!!!

ラーメンじゃないいけれど

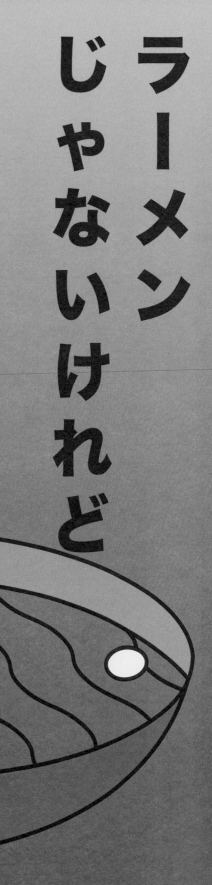

Lazy Goat Ragù-Men

ヤギカレーの
「ラグー麺」
Yagi Karē no 'Ragū-men'

The dish we became most known for at Nanban was what we called the Lazy Goat Ragù-Men, which went through many iterations before winding up in its final form. A former manager suggested the name 'lazy goat' because it no longer really resembled Jamaican curry goat that initially inspired it, and to emphasise how soft and tender the meat was. I came up with 'ragù-men' to signal that it wasn't a typical ramen, with something like a sauce rather than a broth.

It was a so-so performer on the menu until *Time Out* quite unreasonably named it the best dish in London in 2019. I don't think that accolade was at all deserved, but I do love this dish – it has always felt like a real collaboration, something that could only have come to exist by engaging with our customers, our staff and with Brixton Market itself. It's a hyper-local bowl of ramen, very much of particular place and a particular moment. It's weird, complicated, silly and inauthentic – and it's probably the dish I'm most proud of in my entire career.

Makes 4 servings

Curry

1.2 kg (2 lb 11 oz) goat leg (this is the total weight, with the bones and fat and everything; if you're using trimmed goat it'll be more like 1 kg (2 lb 4 oz)

2 onions, roughly chopped

100 g (3.5 oz) (about 2 medium) tomatoes

15 g (0.5 oz) fresh ginger root (peeled weight), thinly sliced against the grain to break up its fibres

10 g (0.35 oz) red Scotch bonnet chilli

vegetable oil, as needed for searing

3 tablespoons hot Madras curry powder

5 g (0.2 oz) cinnamon (cassia) bark

½ tablespoon ground coriander

½ tablespoon gochugaru

1 teaspoon mild Jamaican curry powder

3 cardamom pods, smashed with the blunt side of a knife

2 star anise

10 g (0.35 oz) kombu

500 ml (17 fl oz) chicken stock

300 ml (10 fl oz) water, or more, as needed

gochujang, to taste

shōyu, to taste

Preheat the oven to 150°C fan (350°F).

First, make the curry. Trim up the goat leg by removing most of the thick, yellowish-white fat that runs through the leg, and cutting the meat into big chunks, about 5 cm (2 in) across. Discard the fat but keep any bones. Combine the onions, tomatoes, ginger and Scotch bonnet in a blender or food processor and blitz to a rough purée. Pour a glug of vegetable oil into a deep casserole (Dutch oven) and set over a medium-high heat, then fry the goat chunks until brown on all sides. Do this in batches (otherwise they'll steam rather than sear) and remove each chunk when they're nicely coloured.

Lower the heat to medium and add the onion and tomato mixture. Stir well, scraping up any bits of goat that may have stuck to the bottom of the pot. Cook for about 10 minutes until the mixture begins to colour and no longer has a 'raw onion' smell. Add all of the spices along with a big splash of water, stir and cook for another 5 minutes. If they get too dry and start to catch, just add a bit more water. Break up the kombu into small-ish pieces (about 5–8 cm/2–3¼ in across). Add this to the pot along with the seared goat (and goat bones, if you have them), the chicken stock and the water. Stir well. The liquid should cover the goat; if it doesn't, add a bit more water. Place a piece of baking parchment on the surface of the curry, then cover the casserole with a lid (or some foil). Whack it in the oven. It'll take about 3–4 hours to cook, but start checking it after 2 hours, and stir it periodically to ensure even cooking. Keep checking the goat every hour or so until it is quite soft – when it can be easily torn with chopsticks or tongs, or cut with a spoon, it's done.

→

To assemble

4 portions noodles (Thick and Soft work best, page 78)

shichimi tōgarashi

Seafood Sawdust (page 139)

4 Tea Eggs (page 132)

fried shallots (see method, page 146)

spring onions (scallions), thinly sliced

Separate the meat from the liquid with a slotted spoon and leave the meat to cool until it's no longer too hot to handle. Remove the whole spices, goat bones and kombu, and discard. While the meat is still warm, break up any big chunks (nothing should be bigger than bite-sized) while removing any squishy pockets of fat or tough bits of connective tissue. Whisk a few big spoonfuls of gochujang and shōyu into the gravy and taste; add more of each or both if you want it spicier/sweeter/saltier. Add the picked meat back to the liquid. Reheat to serve.

To serve, have your curry goat hot and ready. Bring a large pan of water to a rolling boil and add the noodles. Cook and drain according to the guide on page 166. Transfer to deep bowls and top with the curry, then the garnishes. Stir everything well before tucking in.

Ponzu Reimen

 Reimen is a dish of noodles in chilled soup, typically referring to Korean *naengmyeon* and its Japanese offshoots. The original Korean version uses buckwheat starch noodles (different from Japanese soba), but in Japan it is also made from wheat noodles such as udon or ramen. It is still mostly the purview of Korean restaurants in Japan, but it also appears on ramen shop menus in the summertime, in attempts to lure customers in on hot, muggy days when steaming broths don't have much appeal. This version uses ponzu as its base, doubling down on the inherent refreshing quality of the dish with zesty citrus aroma and acidity.

BROTH
Any dashi or
 chintan, chilled

TARE
Ponzu
 (see recipe)

NOODLES
Soba-Ramen
 Hybrid

OILS
Garlic Sesame
 or Chilli

TOPPINGS
Cucumber
 and radishes,
 julienned
Sesame seeds
Steamed chicken
 (see recipe) or
 silken tofu
Spring onions
 (scallions)
Cress

OPTIONAL TOPPINGS
Ajitama
 (ramen egg)
 or boiled egg

Makes 2 servings

Ponzu

zest from 2–3 tart citrus fruits (whatever you're using for juice), very finely grated
2 tablespoons dashi
2 tablespoons caster (superfine) sugar
1 tablespoon mirin
¼ teaspoon MSG
¼ teaspoon salt
5 tablespoons lemon, lime, bergamot or yuzu juice (you can use just one, or mix any or all of the four)
5 tablespoons shōyu
2 teaspoons rice vinegar

Steamed chicken

2 tablespoons sake
1 tablespoon shōyu
1 tablespoon mirin
1 cm (½ in) chunk of fresh ginger root, thinly sliced
1 chicken breast, cut into 2 thick goujons

For the ponzu, combine the citrus zest, dashi, sugar and mirin in a small saucepan and warm until steaming. Remove from the heat and stir in the MSG and salt until they dissolve. Leave to cool, then add the remaining ingredients and stir. Pass through a sieve and keep in the refrigerator until ready to use.

For the chicken, stir together the sake, shōyu, mirin and ginger in a microwave-safe container, then add the chicken. Loosely cover the container with a lid or cling film (plastic wrap) and microwave for 3–4 minutes, turning the chicken once halfway through cooking, until just cooked through. (If the chicken is still raw after 4 minutes, keep cooking in 30 second intervals until totally done.) Leave to cool, then shred the meat into bite-size pieces and leave in the steaming liquid, in the refrigerator until ready to use.

To plate, cook the noodles according to the guide on page 166, but cook them softer than you would normally for ramen, because they will firm up when you chill them. As soon as the noodles are done, rinse them well with cold water, then transfer to bowls. Add 60 ml (4 tablespoons) of ponzu to each bowl and add the chilled broth, along with the cucumber, radish, sesame seeds and just a few drops of oil (this dish is all about refreshment, so too much oil will feel out of place). Top with the shredded chicken, spring onions, cress and egg (if using).

NOTE
Shop-bought ponzu is fine for this, as long as you use a good brand.

Frozen Watermelon and Kimchi Reimen

Is there anything more refreshing than watermelon? Frozen watermelon is the only thing that comes to mind. This chilled ramen (*page 199*), or reimen, counters the sweetness of watermelon with hot, zingy kimchi, for a bowlful that cools you down first with its icy broth, then with the beads of sweat that form as you eat more of it.

Makes 2 servings

300 g (10.6 oz) watermelon, deseeded (weight with rind removed), plus a little more, to garnish

300 ml (10 fl oz) kombu dashi (from a powder is fine)

2 tablespoons gochujang

1 tablespoon shōyu

1 tablespoon rice vinegar

juice of 1 lime

a handful of mangetout (snow peas), julienned

2 portions noodles (shop-bought or Soba-Ramen Hybrid, page 82)

100 g (3.5 oz) kimchi, drained and coarsely chopped

150 g (5.3 oz) soft tofu, cubed

2 teaspoons olive oil

a few leaves of mint, shiso or coriander (cilantro), finely sliced

a few pinches of sesame seeds

Cut some of the watermelon into two little triangles, about 1 cm (½ in) thick and reserve these for a garnish. Cut the remaining 300 g (10.6 oz) watermelon into cubes and transfer to a food processor or blender along with the dashi, gochujang, shōyu, vinegar and lime juice. Blend until fairly smooth, then pour into a container and transfer to the freezer. Leave there until the liquid is partially frozen but still mostly liquid. Depending on your freezer situation, this could take anywhere from 30 minutes to a couple of hours, so keep an eye on it.

Blanch the mangetout in boiling water for about a minute, then run under cold water to stop the cooking. Boil the noodles according to the guide on page 166, but cook them softer than you would normally for ramen, because they will firm up when you chill them. As soon as the noodles are done, rinse them well with cold water, then transfer to bowls. Pour over the semi-frozen watermelon broth and stir the noodles through, then top with the kimchi, tofu, mangetout, olive oil, herbs, sesame seeds and watermelon triangles.

ラーメン味の
ソーセージロール

Ramen Aji no Sōsēji Rōru

The Ramen Sausage Roll

 I entered these in a sausage roll competition in 2014, and lost. I'm not usually a sore loser but I am still a little mad about that, because these are really good, damn it. I'll take crispy noodles over greasy pastry any day of the week!

Makes 2 rolls

150 g (5.3 oz) minced (ground) pork

50 g (1.75 oz) cooked chāshū, diced

30 g (1 oz) beni shōga, finely chopped

2 spring onions (scallions), finely chopped

2 tablespoons panko

1 tablespoon miso

1 tablespoon shōyu

1 tablespoon sesame seeds

½ teaspoon sesame oil

¼ teaspoon white pepper

2 garlic cloves, finely chopped

2 portions noodles (thinner noodles are best, and nothing too curly)

oil, as needed for deep-frying

Combine everything except the noodles and oil and mix well. Form into two sausages, about 2.5 cm (1 in) thick, and wrap each one tightly in cling film (plastic wrap), with the ends tied like sweet wrappers, and leave to rest in the refrigerator for 1 hour. Cook the noodles and rinse them well under cold running water, then lay them out straight in a single layer on a cutting board or clean work surface. Unwrap the sausages and position them along one end of each bed of noodles. Roll the sausages up in the noodles, then re-wrap them tightly in cling film, and leave to rest in the refrigerator for another 30 minutes. Pour enough oil into a deep saucepan to come up to a depth of at least 5 cm (2 in) and heat it to 160°C (325°F). Lower in the sausages and fry until well browned and cooked through, about 8 minutes, turning often to ensure even cooking. Drain on paper towels and leave to cool for 5 minutes or so before slicing and serving. These are delicious with hot mustard or tonkatsu sauce, or mayo mixed with some chilli oil.

ラーメンじゃないけれど

ニンニク胡麻味噌 ドレッシングの冷やし中華

Ninnniku Goma Miso Doresshingu no Hiyashi Chūka

Garlic Sesame Miso Ramen Salad

Ramen salad, or *hiyashi chūka*, is a delicious alternative to actual ramen when the mind demands noodles but the body demands cool refreshment. This recipe translates some of the key flavours of a good miso ramen into a rich yet tangy dressing, making it (almost) as moreish and satisfying as the hot version.

Makes 2 servings

Dressing

1 tablespoon sesame oil	
6 garlic cloves, peeled and crushed with the side of a knife	
10 g (0.35 oz) ginger, peeled and finely chopped	
2 tablespoons sesame seeds, plus extra to garnish	
20 g (0.7 oz) sesame paste	
20 g (0.7 oz) white miso	
20 g (0.7 oz) sugar	
2 tablespoons water	
1 tablespoon rice vinegar	
1 tablespoon shōyu	
2 tablespoons yuzu or lime juice	

Salad

8–10 cherry tomatoes	
a small spoonful of shōyu	
2 portions noodles, cooked and chilled with cold water	
½ cucumber, julienned	
½ carrot, shredded	
4 slices cold chāshū or ham, cut into strips, and/or 1 cooked chicken thigh, shredded	
60–70 g (2–2.5 oz) Menma (page 150)	
2 Ajitama (ramen eggs, page 127), or boiled eggs	
1 spring onion (scallion), thinly sliced	
½ sheet nori, cut into little squares	

To make the dressing, heat the sesame oil in a small saucepan over a medium-low heat and add the garlic and ginger. Slowly fry them, tossing occasionally, for about 12 minutes until the garlic is richly coloured on the outside and soft throughout. Remove from the heat and leave to cool. Blitz the sesame seeds to a sandy texture in a food processor, then add the garlic, ginger and oil from the pan (use a spatula to make sure you get all of it) and all the other ingredients. Purée until a rough dressing forms.

Preheat the grill (broiler) to high and arrange the cherry tomatoes on a baking tray. Drizzle each one with a little bit of shōyu, then grill (broil) for about 10 minutes until slightly charred. Leave to cool while you prepare the rest of the salad. When the tomatoes are cool, remove their skins (they should slip off easily). To serve, toss the noodles with about half of the dressing, then place the noodles into wide, shallow bowls. Top with the cucumber, carrot, meat and menma, then pour over the rest of the sauce. Garnish with the tomatoes, eggs, spring onion, nori and a pinch of sesame seeds.

ラーメンじゃないけれど

チキンシーザー
冷やし中華

Chikin Shīzā Sarada no Hiyashi Chūka

Chicken Caesar Ramen Salad

Chicken Caesar salads are often maligned by insufferable foodies on the grounds that chicken doesn't belong in a Caesar salad, like the Caesar salad is something so perfect and pristine that to introduce a piece of chicken to it is an act of vandalism. Whatever. I'm going to take it one step further and add noodles to it, because you know what? Noodles make everything better.

Makes 2 servings

Croutons

4 × 1 cm (½ in) thick slices baguette

1 tablespoon olive oil

½ garlic clove

sea salt, as needed

Dressing

1 egg yolk

½ small garlic clove, finely grated

20 g (0.7 oz) miso

10 g (0.35 oz) Parmesan, finely grated, plus extra to garnish

½ teaspoon katsuo dashi powder

½ teaspoon English mustard

a grind or two of pepper

juice of ½ lemon

½ teaspoon sesame oil

1 tablespoon olive oil

100 ml (3.5 fl oz) vegetable oil

Salad

2 portions noodles, cooked and chilled under cold water

1 chicken breast, cooked and shredded (the Shiokōji Chicken recipe works well here (page 119)

1 head cos (romaine) lettuce, chopped

a big pinch of sesame seeds

a few grinds of black pepper

a handful of chives, thinly sliced

For the croutons, preheat the oven to 180°C fan (400°F). Brush each slice of baguette with olive oil and then rub them with the garlic and season each one with a little sea salt. Cook directly on the rack of the oven for about 15 minutes until toasted and dried out. Remove from the oven and leave to cool, then break into small pieces.

For the dressing, whisk together the egg yolk, garlic, miso, Parmesan, dashi powder, mustard, pepper and lemon juice in a very large bowl (you'll be tossing the whole salad in this bowl). Combine the oils in a jug, then slowly drizzle the oil into the egg yolk mixture while whisking constantly to emulsify. Keep drizzling and whisking until all of the oil is incorporated and you have a thick, creamy dressing. Tip in the noodles, chicken and lettuce and toss well. Serve in wide, shallow bowls garnished with the croutons, sesame seeds, black pepper, Parmesan and chives.

ラーメンじゃないけれど

Not Quite Ramen

揚げ茄子のユーシアン
（魚香）和え油そば
Age-Nasu no Yū Shian Ae Aburasoba

Yu Xiang Aubergine
Mixed Noodles

Aburasoba, or 'oil noodles', is a soupless ramen dish in which the noodles are served in a bowl with tare and oil on the bottom and toppings on top, to be mixed together with chopsticks at the table. The particulars of the dish can vary quite a bit, but it is typically eaten with chilli oil and vinegar. A similar dish is called mazesoba (mixed noodles), which some say is basically the same dish, but from my perspective mazesoba is a distinctly more extravagant dish. It has far more toppings (so many, in fact, that the noodles are often not even visible underneath them), and uses mince (ground meat) and fish powder as key ingredients.

So what is this? It's a mixed noodle dish, with an abundance of toppings, but probably not enough to be called a mazesoba by most noodle nerds. Also, the topping – tangy, sticky, soy saucy Sichuanese *yu xiang* aubergine (eggplant) – contains a good glug of vinegar, and it can indeed be served with chilli oil. So, I'm tempted to call it an aburasoba ... but it would not resemble any aburasoba I've seen in Japan. Aw heck, let's just say it's mixed noodles and call it a day! The aubergine recipe, by the way, is based on one from *Made With Lau*, one of my favourite Chinese recipe blogs that I encourage you to seek out.

→

Serves 2

1 large or 2 small dried
shiitake mushrooms

150 ml (5 fl oz) just-boiled water

1 large aubergine (eggplant)

oil, as needed for shallow-frying

1 teaspoon cornflour (cornstarch)

2 tablespoons shōyu

1 tablespoon dark red miso
(such as Hatchō miso)

1 tablespoon oyster sauce

2 tablespoons Chinkiang vinegar,
Japanese black vinegar or similar,
plus extra to taste

1 red (bell) pepper or a handful of
small, sweet peppers, thinly sliced

2 garlic cloves, finely chopped

15 g (0.5 oz) fresh ginger root,
peeled and finely chopped

1–2 dried red chillies, or a few
pinches of chilli (hot pepper) flakes
(to taste)

3 tablespoons light brown sugar

1 tablespoon sesame oil

2 portions noodles (Go-To, Springy-
Chewy, Thick and Soft, Toasted
Sesame or Shop-bought)

2 spring onions (scallions), thinly
sliced at an angle

2 egg yolks or Onsen Eggs (page 134)

50–60 g (1.75–2 oz) Menma (page 150)

chilli oil, to taste

Place the shiitake mushrooms in a small dish and cover them with the boiled water, then leave to rehydrate for about an hour. Meanwhile, cut the aubergine into batons or prisms about 2 cm (¾ in) thick, and pour the oil into a large frying pan or wok to a depth of about 1 cm (½ in). Heat over a medium-high heat for a few minutes, then test the temperature by placing a piece of aubergine into the oil. If it sizzles vigorously immediately, the oil is ready. Add all of the aubergine to the oil and fry for about 5–6 minutes, turning often, until richly browned all over. Remove with a slotted spoon or spider and drain well on paper towels. Tip the oil out into a heatproof container, but leave about 1 tablespoon oil or so in the pan.

Once the mushrooms have rehydrated, remove their stems and cut them into thin slices. Stir the cornflour into the resulting mushroom dashi and stir together the shōyu, miso, oyster sauce and vinegar in a separate bowl until no lumps of miso remain.

Ensure you have all of your prep ready to go before cooking, because the pace needs to be fairly quick once you begin. Place the pan with the reserved 1 tablespoon oil back over a high heat. Once the oil is shimmering, add the peppers and stir-fry for 2–3 minutes until browned. Add the garlic, ginger and chillies, and stir-fry for another 1–2 minutes, then add the sliced shiitake mushrooms and sugar and stir-fry briefly so the sugar melts and bubbles. Add the liquid seasoning mixture and stir well, then add the cornflour and mushroom dashi mixture and bring to the boil so it thickens. Finally, tip in the fried aubergine and stir well to coat. Reduce the heat to low to keep warm while you cook the noodles.

Divide the sesame oil between the two bowls and add a few spoonfuls of the aubergine sauce to each one. Boil the noodles until tender, then drain well and tip into the sauce. Stir the noodles through the sauce, then top with the aubergine and its sauce, and garnish with the spring onions, eggs and menma. Serve with chilli oil and extra vinegar – add as much as you like.

Not Quite Ramen

WHAT TO DO WITH LEFTOVER INGREDIENTS AND OTHER RAMEN-ADJACENT IDEAS
残り材料の使い方
NOKORI ZAIRYŌ NO TSUKAIKATA

The Ramen Burger

Full credit to legendary ramen chef Keizo Shimamoto for inventing this what feels like decades ago now. Essentially, Keizo formed cooked noodles into a circular disc, which then sets into a puck upon chilling. The pucks are then lightly griddled to develop colour and texture on the outside, and used as buns for burgers made with various Japanese seasonings and toppings. I had the good fortune of trying one of these in Brooklyn probably about 10 years ago now, and as an avid fan of both ramen and burgers, I can attest that it was fabulous.

The Ramen Sandwich

This is sort of an inversion of the ramen burger, which I first learned about from chef Milli Taylor. Basically, you cook noodles, slick them with melted butter, season them (a dry seasoning like the powder packet from instant ramen works best) and stuff them between two slices of white bread. Sillier and simpler than the ramen burger, but potentially even more delicious.

Rice: Ramen Risotto, Chāshū Chāhan, Chāshū Don, Takikomi Gohan

Ramen ingredients make excellent rice dishes. The broth can be used to make risotto or *takikomi gohan* (rice cooked with various seasonings), while the toppings, especially odds and ends of chāshū, makes great fried rice or donburi.

Crispy Noodles: Snacks and Desserts

If you deep-fry ramen noodles, they go super crispy and develop a flavour like pretzels, which makes sense because those are also treated with an alkaline solution before baking. These can be used as a garnish for salads, or put in a snack mix à la Bombay mix, or used to add crunch to creamy desserts such as sundaes.

Cocktails

Cocktails that verge on savoury can incorporate ramen ingredients, like a dash or two of shio tare in a dry martini or some mushroom dashi in a Manhattan. But my favourite cocktail to ramen-ise is easily the Bloody Mary, which can incorporate shōyu or miso tare; aroma oils such as garlic sesame or chilli oil; and other Japanese seasonings such as wasabi, tonkatsu sauce, yuzu or yuzu-koshō and shichimi. They can also be garnished with toppings like ajitama, chāshū, menma and nori.

What to Do with Leftover Ingredients

ラーメンじゃないけれど

RESOURCES
推奨読書
SUISHŌ DOKUSHO

The amount of information on ramen in English has absolutely exploded in the past decade, and there are now numerous books, blogs and Instagram accounts that are incredibly useful for understanding the finer points of ramen. The books I'd most recommend are:

Let's Make Ramen! by Hugh Amano and Sarah Becan
Ramen Otaku by Sarah Gavigan
Ivan Ramen by Ivan Orkin
Momofuku by David Chang (an oldie but a goodie)
Slurp! A Social and Culinary History of Ramen by Dr Barak Kushner

However, by far the most comprehensive and useful book I know of on the subject is actually a free e-book, *The Ramen_Lord Book of Ramen* by Mike 'ramen_lord' Satinover and his brother Scott Satinover. The book takes a very detailed, scholarly approach and goes deep into the 'why' of ramen, rather than just the 'how'.

The other book I relied upon the most for research was Ryōichi Nishio's incomparable *Ramen Taizen*, which also has the English title *The Complete Ramen*, though the book does not have an English edition. If you don't read Japanese, get it anyway and just bust out the camera function on the Google Translate app. There's some amazing information in there.

Of course, books are just part of the ramen knowledge base. There's still a lot more information online than there is in print, in both English and Japanese. I have learned a ton from the following Instagram accounts:

Cody Mizuno (@ramenguidejapan)
Elvin Yung (@shikaku.ramen)
David Chan (@nichijou.ramen)
James Chant (@matsudairamen)

As well as the following blogs and YouTube channels:
ramenbeast.com
wayoframen.com
yapparimengasuki.com
youtube.com/@OutimenTV.
youtube.com/@ramenrotas

Keep reading,
keep watching,
keep slurping,
keep learning.
The path to ramen perfection
may be never-ending,
but it's not a lonely road.

ACKNOWLEDGEMENTS
謝辞
SHAJI

I'm really up against the maximum word count here, so forgive this terse and impersonal list of all of the wonderful people who have worked on this book or otherwise supported me and made this possible! Holly Arnold, Emma Hopkin, Eila Purvis, Kajal Mistry, Esme Curtis, Emiko Pitman, Laura Edwards, Jo Cowan, Matthew Hague, Tamara Vos, Rachel Vere, Evi O, Miho Oguri, Morgan Pitelka, Motoko Ezaki, Laura Anderson, James Chant, Rivaaj Maharaj and Patrick Foster. Thank you all!

ABOUT THE AUTHOR
著者について
CHOSHA NITSUITE

Tim Anderson is a chef and author who has been making ramen professionally for 10 years, and has been making reasonably good ramen for approximately three of those years. He ran the ramen restaurant Nanban in London from its inception as a pop-up in 2012 until he exited the business in 2021 to focus on his family and his writing.

Anderson has pursued an interest in Japanese food for more than two decades, first as a hobby, then as a student, then as a career. In 2005 he was awarded a research grant to study local foods in Japan centred on the Shin-Yokohama Ramen Museum. After relocating to London in 2008, he has gone on to win *MasterChef* on BBC1, in which he cooked ramen as part of his final meal. He has since written six previous books on Japanese cookery, including *Your Home Izakaya* and *JapanEasy*. He currently lives in South London with his wife Laura, daughter Tig, son Felix and FIV-positive cat Baloo. Anderson is also a recently accredited humanist funeral celebrant.

His favourite Marvel film remains *Spider-Man: Into the Spider-Verse* and his favourite Marvel TV show is *Luke Cage*.

Index

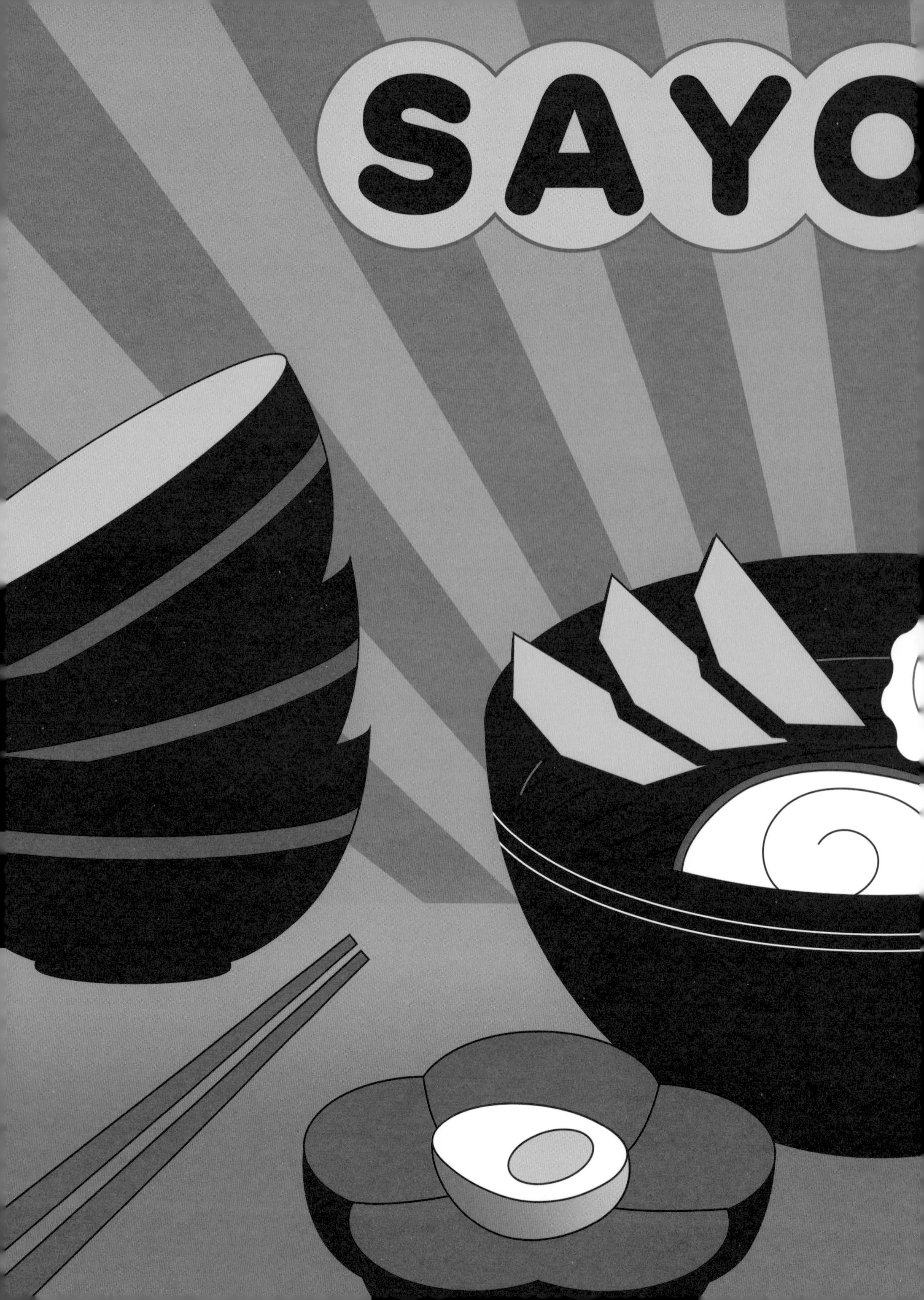
SAYO

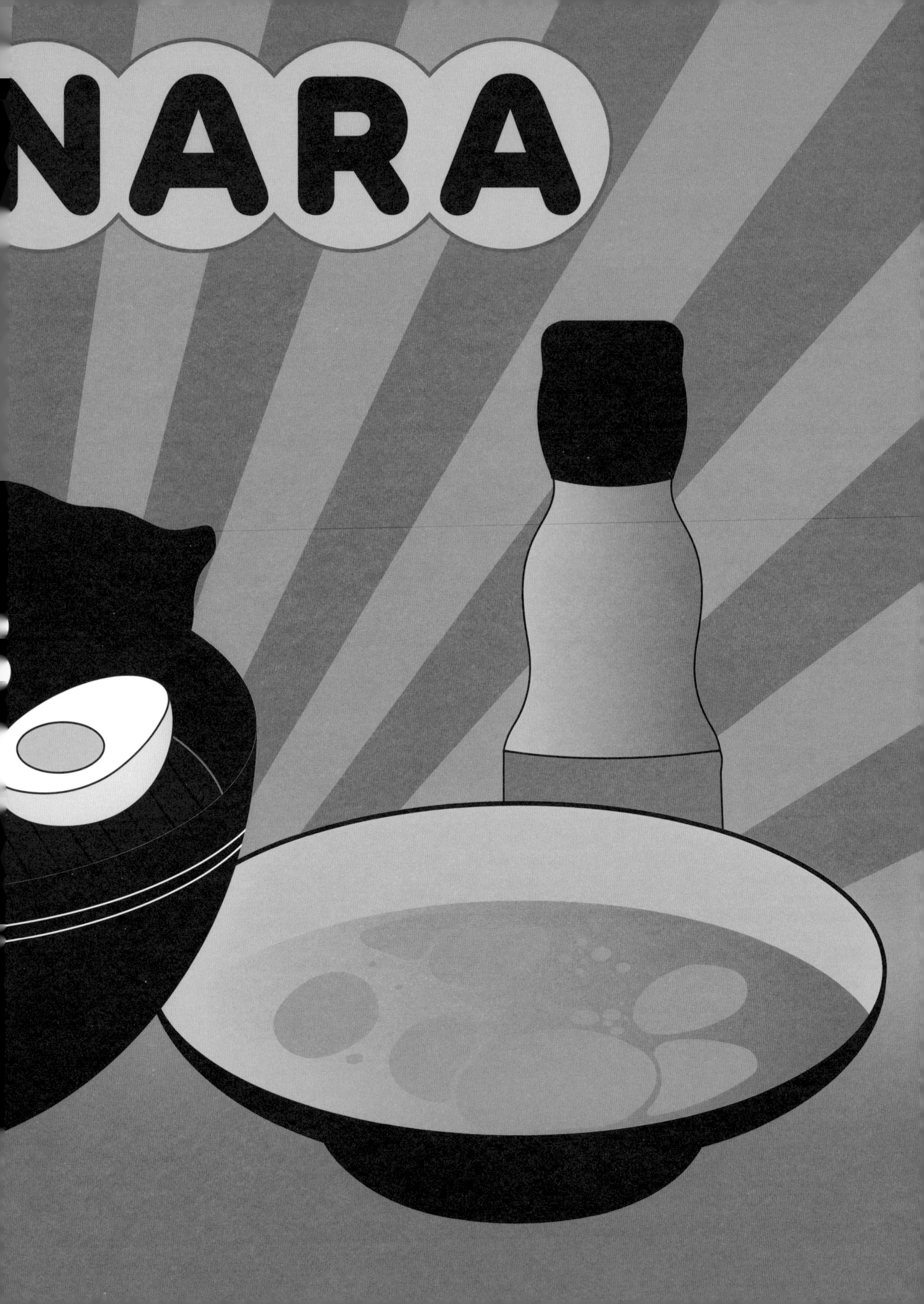
NARA

Published in 2023 by Hardie Grant Books,
an imprint of Hardie Grant Publishing

Hardie Grant Books (London)
5th & 6th Floors
52–54 Southwark Street
London SE1 1UN

Hardie Grant Books (Melbourne)
Building 1, 658 Church Street
Richmond, Victoria 3121

hardiegrantbooks.com

Text © Tim Anderson
Photography © Laura Edwards
Illustrations © Evi-O Studio

British Library Cataloguing-in-Publication Data. A catalogue
record for this book is available from the British Library.

Ramen Forever
ISBN: 978-178488-660-8

10 9 8 7 6 5 4 3

Publishing Director: Kajal Mistry
Acting Publishing Director: Emma Hopkin
Senior Editor: Eila Purvis
Design and Art Direction: Evi-O Studio | Evi O.
Illustrations: Siena Zadro, Emi Chiba and Evi O.
Food Stylist: Tamara Vos
Prop Sylist: Rachel Vere
Copy-editor: Esme Curtis
Proofreader: Kathy Steer
Production Controller: Katie Jarvis

Colour reproduction by p2d
Printed and bound in China by Leo Paper Products Ltd.